THE
AMISH COOK
EDITOR'S

EVERYTHING BUT THE
KITCHEN SINK BOOK

KEVIN WILLIAMS

LIMITED EDITION PRINT RUN - 2010

ABOUT THE KITCHEN SINK

Prior to World War II, most sinks - kitchen and bathroom - were stainless steel. The alloy was durable with the frequent use and, well, that was just the way it always had been. But as a steel shortage began to plague the defense industry, companies began switching metals. So items like the copper penny became the zinc penny (copper was used in munitions) and stainless steel sinks became ceramic. In fact, this is where the term "everything but the kitchen sink" originated, where basically metals - including the kitchen sink - went into the US war arsenal. In recent years, stainless steel has once again been finding its way into kitchen and bathroom sinks. Most Amish homes tend to feature stainless steel sinks. So the expression "everything but the kitchen sink" has come to mean a hodge-podge of a little bit of everything. This book lives up to its title offering a little bit of everything Amish. There is some first person narrative in this book, some "I" and "myself," those are referring to me - your guide and Amish Cook editor — Kevin Williams.

This book was put together as an "all under one roof" guide to anything Amish. I felt like we could have kept on working and working and working on it, but one has to draw the line somewhere. Hmmm, maybe someday there will be a "Kitchen Sink", Vol II.☺ Enjoy the journey!

COMING SOON: NOT SO SIMPLE

The Amish Cook column has captured the hearts of millions of readers for almost 20 years in newspapers across the country and now online. But what's the story *behind* the story? Soon, you'll find out. For the first time, the column's editor, Kevin Williams, tells readers how the column *really* began, shares the struggles of keeping it going, and all along the journey you'll meet a colorful cast of characters from Old Order Mennonite buggy-makers in Virginia to Amish bakers in nestled in the hills of Adams County, Ohio to plain German Baptists perched high in the foothills of the Sierra Nevada. It's a journey that spans a continent, several centuries, and multiple faiths.

Ultimately the story is one of persistence, perseverance and, in the end, embracing simplicity. Following is a special preview:

NOT SO SIMPLE: My journey among the Amish, Mennonites, and Other Plain People, and the story of the most popular newspaper column you've probably never read.

PROLOGUE

My fingers fumble with the stubborn latch swinging from the end of a long rusty chain. I can tell by the way the lock protests that this place receives few visitors. It's not something the Amish do. But I'm not Amish. All of the souls here are, or were, though. This is a walk I've made several times now and on each occasion I feel uneasy and rushed, as if I'm planting a flag on the moon and then sprinting back to the safety of my spacecraft. I'm dressed in jeans, t-shirt and flip-flops, alien attire in these parts. I mean no disrespect by my casual clothes; this wasn't a planned visit. I found myself in the area and was drawn to the cemetery by the magnetic pull of unresolved emotions. So I abandoned my car down by the shoulder of the road and scrambled up the cemetery hill. Horse-drawn buggies, the color of funeral crepe, occasionally pass in both directions on the paved road that runs in front of the graveyard. I sense the stares from under straw hats and black bonnets, but I ignore them. I am allowed to be here, I tell myself.

I lift and then heave open the paddock door, which issues a curdling groan seemingly announcing to the entire surrounding Amish settlement that I'm here. I lope up the grassy incline of the paddock, where horses graze placidly during funerals, their hooves leaving the turf clumpy and uneven. I arrive at a second gate where my fingers, covered with flecks of rust residue from the first latch, go to work again. As I squeeze the decrepit clasp, I look around and stop. No one there. I always feels like I'm being watched, but other than curious eyes peering from passing buggies, I never see anyone. Far beyond the cemetery's back split-rail fence is a two-story, white farmhouse, encircled by rippling fields of delicately tended hay and soybeans. I imagine a stern, bearded Amish man inside the home watching me through binoculars, shaking his head disapprovingly. But I see nothing of the sort.

For a long time I did not come back. The Amish make it easy not to. Their cemeteries aren't likes ours: no bright, cheery flowers, teddy bears, wreaths, bubbling fountains, or peaceful paths. Amish cemeteries are usually invisible, without even tombstones, just lumpy earth and wooden markers etched with the initials of the deceased.

My first time here was a surreal, slow-motion swirl of somber faces, bushy beards, whispered words and wide-brimmed Sunday hats. When I close my eyes I can hear the crisp sound of finality in the clods of dirt being dropped spade by spade onto the casket. Then there was the media. On the evening after her death, *The New York Times* kept calling me during supper, the fact-checker wanting to make sure various dates and names were correct. Then it was the *Wall Street Journal* fishing for a colorful quote or two. The next day when I was seeking a lunch refuge at a Chinese buffet, it was the *Los Angeles Times* and *San Francisco Chronicle* calling me between bites of vegetable lo mein. Nighttime brought the news crawler at the bottom of CNN announcing my friend's death. She had become quite well known for her newspaper column. Part of all the attention, I'd be lying if I said otherwise, was gratifying. After all, the media – at least for a moment – had noticed us. Of course part of me was resentful that it took a death for them to call, but at least they were calling. Then, as quickly as they came, the media vanished and it was quiet and my life continued its perplexing hopscotch through America's plain communities.

So here I stand in this serene, nameless graveyard almost a decade later. The cemetery is higher in elevation than almost any other point in the area, a panoramic ridge of relief where a cleansing wind seems to carry my sins away. Across the road I can see a one-room schoolhouse, where Amish children spill out for afternoon recess in a pin-wheeling blur of bonnets and straw hats. It's like a scene from so many of the Amish calendars sold in mall kiosks. In another direction, a towering windmill spins like a roulette wheel in the brisk breeze. I finally push the second gate, which gives with more silent resistance than the first and suddenly I'm inside. The spongy soil sinks beneath my feet. I'm drawn to a far corner of this resting place for the dead and that's where I find it. Two initials - "E.C." - are etched in a now aging wooden grave-marker. In fact, all of the headstones here, true to tradition, are only inscribed with initials. The letters I'm staring at stand for "Elizabeth Coblentz," but she wouldn't want people to know. The Amish prefer to die as they live, unassuming and of the earth. I squat and trace my fingers across the top of the low wooden marker, as if somehow I can connect with her by touching a rotting slab of timber.

INTRODUCTION

My journey began on July 12, 1986 in an Ohio hollow with a block of cheese and a loaf of bread.

Outsiders think of Ohio as a land of cornfields, Buckeyes, and boredom. But there's a hidden part of the state that most people – even those that live here – don't often see. It's as if West Virginia and Kentucky's Appalachia at some point became too full and spilled its contents into neighboring southeastern Ohio, painting our state's familiar flatness with craggy ridges, deep coves, meandering black bear, and impenetrable forests. In winter, this hill country gets pummeled with snowstorms that swirl up from the south. During summer, the area soaks in the oppressively humid haze of an Appalachian afternoon. It was while passing through this untamed, unfamiliar Ohio that a block of cheese and a loaf of bread changed the path of my life, although at the time I certainly didn't realize this was happening.

I was a bored almost 14-year-old boy watching the world pass from the back of my parents' Oldsmobile. I wasn't interested in the area's topography or history: I just wanted the drive to be over, to arrive at our North Carolina beachfront hotel where seven days of sand, saltwater, and teenage girls awaited. But my reverie was interrupted by Mom excitedly exclaiming something followed by Dad pulling over to the shoulder of the road, stirring up a cyclone of gravel and dust in his haste.

To call it a roadside stand would actually be a bit of glamorization. It wasn't much more than a black buggy parked in a patch of grass alongside the road. A few tables filled with crumb-top apple pies, layer cakes dripping with icing, and stacks of golden sugar cookies surrounded the buggy. A copper-colored horse was tied to a nearby tree munching on handfuls of hay that had been dumped on the ground. Up until this screeching stop I had never even *heard* of the Amish, let alone seen any. I was immediately fascinated by the 19th century daguerreotype before me.

"They live like people did back in the 1800s," was my father's abbreviated and oversimplified explanation as he steadied the car to a stop.

I'm a born Buckeye, but just a few years earlier, my father's job in international steel sales had me spending most of my childhood in the teeming cities of the Middle East. Abu Dhabi, capital of the United Arab Emirates, an oil-soaked fiefdom on the tip of Arabia's boot, was one of the sandy desert outposts where we lived for a time. Abu Dhabi is the more practical, less glamorous city-state stepsister to preening, chest-pounding Dubai with its opulent western-style malls and its famous (or infamous) man-made palm-tree shaped island. Abu Dhabi was, and still is, a city struggling to find its identity. The crowded city-state was a swirl of cultures all clamoring for an economic and social foothold. Expatriates of every ethnicity streamed into the emirate hoping for one of the coveted construction jobs that each one of the Sheik's pet projects seemed to require. And while it was often impossible to navigate all the cultural customs, from Afghan to Uzbek to Arabian to Persian, I quickly learned that food was a language we all spoke. Barriers would crumble while sharing feasts of tahini-soaked *hummus*, laughs would be enjoyed over a Lebanese eggplant dish called *baba ghanoush*, and friendships forged over *shwarma*, a hot meat sandwich spiced with mint and soaked in a yogurt sauce. We made fast friends with a family from India who plied us with homemade French fries and honey-soaked spheres of deep-fried dough known as *gulab jamun*. But we just called them honey balls.

It was Wednesday nights, however, that captured my culinary and cultural imagination. That's when an elderly Afghan woman living and working in a lean-to in the achingly impoverished bazaar (locals called them *souks*) would fire loaves of flatbread in a round stone oven. A single bare light bulb dangled flimsily from the ceiling of the bakery, its dim rays bouncing off the dull blue walls. The slight wisp of a woman, almost completely obscured by her thick black burqa, would pass my father a steaming loaf of flatbread wrapped in a wax paper sleeve. Her aged, twisted hands would then cup to complete the transaction: bread in exchange for a couple of *dirhams*. With wide-eyed awe, I'd watch the collision of cultures: the sight of my fair-skinned, tall, patrician father conducting business with the stooped withered woman in the burqa. And we'd then disappear, out of the souk, across the street and into our apartment tower. Up we would go to the airy affluence of our 13th floor abode where we'd tear off pieces of the bread while it was still warm. Any unconsumed bread would harden into something resembling a bookshelf by the next morning.

Mainly affluent British, Dutch and Americans lived in our high-rise, while the surrounding slums spreading out from the tower's base were populated with economically struggling Arabs, Persians, Pakistanis, Afghans, and Uzbeks. Our apartment had clean running water, electricity, and a new device called a VCR, all amenities only dreamt of in the miasma of surrounding souks and shantytowns. Looking back, I'm sure some of the earliest smoldering resentment towards westerners originated from this colonial economic disparity. Meanwhile the mainly Muslim population outside our towers would find a refuge in religion, answering the mullah's call for prayer as it tumbled sternly out of the minarets, ricocheting across the city below, while we buttered and savored our warm bread inside.

Often, I would take my binoculars and scan the souks from my bedroom window above, sometimes shocked by the parched poverty below. It seemed a galaxy away from my life, but it wasn't, and at times, like when we ventured into the souk for flatbread, our two very different worlds would briefly bump up against one another. Day after day, I was drawn to my bedroom window, mesmerized by what was spread out below: shantytowns, souks, mosques, and roads jammed with coughing cars.

When we did move back to the United States, the Amish and their seemingly anachronistic ways were nowhere on my teenage radar.

Shoofly pie, snickerdoodles, and rhubarb coffeecake were as foreign to me as hummus and *shwarma* would be to most Amish. Places like Abu Dhabi and Dubai, were cultural cauldrons swirling with Pakistanis, English, and Arabs – not Amish. These hubs of international intrigue were far more familiar, and comfortable, to me than Lancaster and Shipshewana. The Amish, however, were capturing the imagination of many other Americans, thanks in large part to an assist from Hollywood. Just a year earlier, in 1985, the Harrison Ford movie, *Witness*, became a box office blockbuster, introducing millions of Americans to Amish ways, even if they were a bit romanticized by starry-eyed screenwriters. I, too occupied with teenage trivialities, was not one of the movie-goers. Mom and Dad, however, had seen *Witness* just months before our North Carolina vacation and maybe that's why they braked for the buggy. Or perhaps they were just captivated by the simple sight of a carriage parked alongside the road.

The Amish entrepreneur running the roadside stand had a broad smile and a lingering black beard, not unlike the ones sported by the most devout Muslims I had lived among just a few years earlier. I peered into the buggy, spying billowy loaves of bread sealed in plastic bags, an assortment of homemade cookies, and a handwritten sign advertising cheese. My mother motioned to the cheese, while my father rummaged through loaves of bread on the table. The Amish man reached into a Coleman cooler for a block of Swiss cheese. It was a minor, meaningless detail, but the fiberglass cooler with its bright green lid seemed oddly out of place in an otherwise undisturbed tableau of ebony and ivory turn-of-the-century simplicity. Then the scene reverted to something more familiar to me: Dad handing, this time a few dollars instead of *dirhams*, to a person dressed in black. And, of course, the black was not a burqa. The man was dressed, as most Amish men dress, in dark denim, suspenders, and a work-shirt. As I watched rapt, the transaction occurred between the Amish man and my father, much like it had between the elderly Afghan woman with the stone oven. I surveyed the simplicity: the horse, the buggy, beard, suspenders, and denim. Deep within I felt a fascination, a tug, a longing of some sort, and then the sensation let go.

To most people the souks and minarets of the Middle East and the bakeries and buggies of the Amish have little, if anything, in common. It took years for me to realize it, but, to me, they had almost everything in common. This eventual epiphany would one day help me resolve some issues in my own life.

Several years later I would learn that the Amish man running the roadside cheese stand was named Roy Bontrager. Mr. Bontrager carefully bagged up the cheese and bread and gave it to Mom. Dad maneuvered the car back onto Ohio Route 32 and we headed back to our vacation. Mom began carving the block of Swiss into soft slices and placing them on the bread. I'm not sure my brother awoke and left the car during the entire stop. I savored the soft goodness of the bread and cheese and then settled into the long drive, the miles melting beneath our car. And, of course, there was no way I could have known it, but this would not be the last time my path would cross with Roy Bontrager's.

Chapter 1

AMISH/ANABAPTIST
DEMOGRAPHIC/REGIONAL INFO

GUIDE TO PLAIN AMERICA - 2010

This is a list of most of the plain settlements in the United States and Canada. This list is not meant to be a comprehensive, exhaustive list of every single settlement. Amish and Mennonite churches are constantly splitting, dividing, and moving so keeping an update-to-date current list of every community is a near impossibility, but this list is quite thorough. This list derives from a combination of information, drawing on personal visits, reading, Amish newspapers, and other sources.

Alabama - Hartselle, Orville

Alaska: Sterling, Wasilla

NORTHERN EXPOSURE: AMISH IN ALASKA?

The Budget newspaper features some writers from Sterling and Wasilla (yes, THAT Wasilla). The letters exude the same plain tone of ones in the Continental 48 and are from Troyers and Millers. It's the same plain voice but with a decidedly Alaskan twist. One writer shares:

"The Iditarod sled dog races are the subject of local talk this week, especially as there are several of the local mushers participating. Of the 71 mushers, a number of them have dropped out for various reasons, an accident, tired dogs, physical sickness, etc."

There is actually not an Amish settlement in Alaska. These writers are conservative Mennonites who have recently moved to the Last Frontier. Might the Amish be next?

In 2009-2010 Amish "advance teams" came to Alaska to scout for suitable land to begin some conservative communities. They left without any deals, but it's probably only a matter of time before the Last Frontier embraces its first Amish residents.

Arizona: Black Canyon City (winter only)

Arkansas: Belleville, Harrison, Huntsville, Mountain View, Nashville, Pocohantas, Salem, Strawberry, Viola

California - Bangor, Lodoc, Modesto (German Baptist)

Colorado: LaJara, Olathe

Connecticut: None

Delaware: Dover

Florida: Blountstown, Lake Butler, Pinecraft

Georgia: Austell, East Dublin, Montezuma, Metter

Hawaii: no plain population

Idaho: Bonners Ferry

Illinois: Anna, Arcola, Arthur, Ava, Barry, Belle River, Bluford, Carrier Mils, Cisne, Clayton, Colchester, Cuba, Dale, Eewing, Flat Rock, Humboldt, Newberry, Olney, Opdyke, Orchardville, Pleasant Hill, Sullivan, Tampico

Indiana: Nappanee-La Grage, Adams County, Fountain City, Wayne County, Greentown-Kokomo, Montgomery

Iowa: Kaloma, Bloomfield, Hazelton

AMANA COLONIES, IOWA

People often ask if the Amana Colonies in Iowa are somehow connected to the Amish. The short answer: they're not. The Amana Colonies were a communal society that had/has its roots in the Pietist movement, the same movement that created the German Baptist Church, which is a "plain church" but distinctly different from the Amish. The Amish-Mennonite-Hutterite religions have their roots in Anabaptism (adult baptismal). Both movements were reactions against the reformation when Martin Luther split from Catholicism, but the pietist movement – while sharing similarites to the Anabaptists - was decidedly different. Anyway, back to the Amana Colonies: The Amana Colonies were a pietist, communal society up until the 1930s, but as the population shrunk and aged out, they then formed the Amana Corporation to oversee the colony's holdings and diversify economically. Today, a CEO oversees it just like a regular company. Today, the Amana Colonies comprise a diverse economic base and are much different from their original agrarian, communal roots.

Kansas: Axtell, Chetopa, Lyndon, Thayer, Yoder, Haven, Hesston, Garnett,

Kentucky: Crofton, Cub Run, Leitchfield, Mays Lick, Munfordville, Upton

Louisiana: None

Maine: Corinna, Oakfield, Smyrna

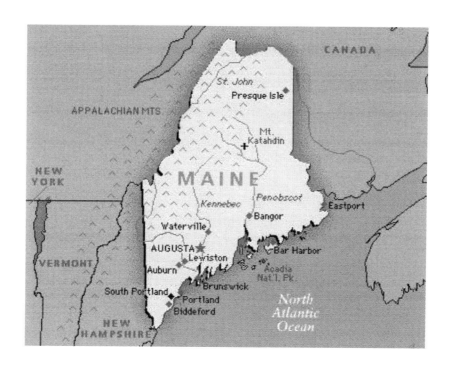

Maryland : Oakland, Swanton

Massachusetts : None

Michigan: Bronson, Camden, Cass City, Centreville, Charlotte, Clare, Gladwin, LeRoy, Manton, Marion, Marlette, Mio, Quincy

Minnesota: Brooten, Clarissa, Collegeville, Fertile, Harmony, Granger, Staples, Utica, Wadena

Special Minnesota Notes: Harmony, in the southeast part of the state, is the largest Minnesota Amish community. The Amish settlement at Collegeville experienced a rare outbreak of polio in 2005, contracted through immunizations. The immunizations use a mild strain of polio to protect against contracting more severe strains. On rare occasions these immunizations can cause a mild form of the disease they are trying to prevent. This happened in central Minnesota's Amish settlement in in 2005. The epidemic, however, was quickly extinguished and everyone recovered.

Mississippi: Macon, Randolph, Saucier, Hot Coffee (Old Order German Baptist Brethren)

Missouri

Montana: Fairfield, Gold Creek, Libby, Lewistown, Rexford, St. Ignatius

Special Montana Notes: The first Old Order Amish settled in Montana in the early 1970s. Up until that point no Amish lived west of Kansas. The initial settlement was Rexford, where the Amish church has thrived ever since. There are now bakeries, furniture shops, and an annual auction for the Amish school. As Rexford has grown, Amish churches have been established in neighboring Washington, Oregon, and Idaho and throughout Montana. One Amish settlement (St. Ignatius) is on an Indian reservation!

Nebraska: Pawnee City, Orchard

Nevada : None

New Hampshire: None

New Jersey: None

New Mexico: Belen

New York: The Empire State's Amish population boasts the fastest growing rate of any state. The biggest growth is occurring in the Mohawk Valley region in the central part of the state. Older settlements are in the far North Country and in the SW near Jamestown. The Amish community outside Jamestown is the largest in the state.

North Carolina: Taylorsville

North Dakota: none

Ohio: Ohio is in pretty much of a statistical tie with Pennsylvania as having the largest population of Old Order Amish of any state. Populations can be found throughout Holmes and Wayne Counties and in the northwest part of the state in Williams County and in the Belle Center area of Ohio. There is a growing Amish settlement in Adams County, Ohio, throughout SE Ohio's Appalachia region, in east-central Ohio near Barnesville, and a new community of Swartzentruber Amish near Sinking Springs.

Oklahoma: Choteau, Colegate, Thomas

Oregon: Harrisburg

Pennsylvania: Pennsylvania's Amish population has declined as Amish have moved to other areas. Still, Lancaster County has a very large Amish population, but Amish can also be found near Shanksville in the SW part of the state, near Meadville, New Wilmington, and in pockets throughout Central PA.

Rhode Island: None

South Carolina: Batesburg, Blackville, Cross Hill

South Dakota: Tripp

Tennessee: Belvidere, Cottage Grove, Crossville, Deer Lodge, Whitesville, Ethridge

Texas: Beeville, Lott, Mexica

Utah: None

Vermont

Virginia: Dayton (Old Order Mennonites), Stuarts Draft (Amish)

Washington: Rochester

West Virginia : Gap Mills, Slanesville

Wisconsin: Pardeeville, Portage, Rhinelander, Cashton,

Wyoming: none

POPULATION BY STATE

Ohio: 49,750

Pennsylvania: 40,100

Indiana: 32,650

Wisconsin: 10,250

Michigan: 9,300

Missouri: 6,100

Kentucky: 5,150

New York: 5,000

Iowa: 4,850

Illinois: 4,200

Minnesota: 1,600

Tennessee: 1,500

Delaware: 1,100

Kansas: 1,100

Maryland: 800

Oklahoma: 700

Montana: 550

Virginia: 550

WHAT'S IN A NAME?

The Amish generally descend from a few dozen founding families. Common last names include: Bontrager, Byler (alt. Beiler), Coblentz, Gingerich, Graber, Keim, Mast, Miller, Schwartz, Shelter, Stutzman, Yoder, and Zook.

Common first names for men: Amos, Eli, Solomon, Jonathan, Daniel, Samuel, Esther, Deborah, Sarah, Joseph, Elizabeth, Moses, Miriam, Aaron, Ezekiel

Common first names for women: Sarah, Irene, Elizabeth, Emma, Mary, Arlene

EDITOR'S FAVORITE AMISH SETTLEMENTS:

PINECRAFT, FLORIDA -

Yes, there is an Amish settlement in Florida. Amish farmers were lured to the west coast of Florida in the 1920s by the promise of profitable celery farms. The celery scheme never really did pan out, but the Amish who ventured down decided to stay. Almost a century later, their early influence survives in the form of Pinecraft, tucked away in a quiet corner of Sarasota.

Sarasota, Florida is like most other Sunshine State cities. The sunny haven features some beautiful beaches, tony shops on nearby Lido Key, and is home to many year-round retirees along with a large winter population of "snowbirds" escaping winter's wrath far to the north. Tucked away in a relatively quiet corner of sprawling Sarasota, however, near the busy intersection of Bahia Vista and Beneva Blvds, is a community known as "Pinecraft." Pinecraft serves as a winter haven for Amish "snowbirds" seeking a warm respite from the harsh midwestern climes. In January and February, Pinecraft is at its peak of activity and a recent day there showed shuffleboard courts full and sidewalks bustling. The post office, Big Olaf's ice cream, and Yoder's restaurant appear to be popular gathering spots for the Amish to catch up with friends and neighbors. Even the Amish newspaper **The Budget** is available for purchase. Troyer's restaurant also does a brisk business, adding a touristy touch to the area.

A mural near the middle of Pinecraft captures an Amish scene from a typical midwestern community and provides residents with an optical taste of home. But the warm air and swaying palm trees in the vicinity - and the occasional alligator - provide ample evidence that "we aren't in Kansas (or Ohio)" anymore.

It's Friday afternoon and an Amish woman in a white prayer cap and solid-colored dress grimaces as she begins pedaling across Beneva Blvd, finally gaining enough speed to sail across to the other side before the light changes. That may be the height of the hard life for the Amish who winter here. Gone - at least for awhile - are the tough mornings of milking, feeding the horses, and collecting eggs from the hen-house. The streets, though, reflect their namesakes up north with names like Graber, Yoder, and Miller. Trees weighed down with heavy ripening grapefruit stand in yards. If one wonders how an occasional recipe for "grapefruit jam" or "grapefruit pie" ends up in the recipe box of an Amish woman in Wisconsin or Illinois, chances are it originated here.

The Amish generally arrive by bus and there are even a few charter lines that cater almost exclusively to the Amish who keep Pinecraft bustling during the winter months.

In addition to becoming a winter haven for the Old Order Amish, Pinecraft has also become a way-station of sorts for Anabaptists who might be exploring other orders. Perhaps an Old Order Amish young person thinking of leaving the strict confines of the church will come to Pinecraft for awhile to explore. An Anabaptist of any age can come here and feel welcome and since newcomers and transients are the norm, few questions are asked. The young wayward teen, Faron, featured in the documentary **Devil's Playground** (a much-talked about, but slightly skewed look at Anabaptist youth) eventually found his way to Sarasota to try out a more liberal life. Either way, whether a person is a strict Swartzentruber or a more liberal Beachy Amish, Pinecraft offers a refuge from some of the rigid rules up north.

"It is much more relaxed here. The Amish have a chance to socialize with people from all orders," says Todd Emrich, who is president of the Pinecraft Neighborhood Association. Shuffleboard is an ardent pasttime among Amish visitors here. "We have eight courts, but we could easily have 16 and keep them full," Emrich says. Emrich's family also runs Yoder's Amish Restaurant.

No one knows exactly how many Amish come to Pinecraft each year, since no formal surveys are taken, but Emrich says about 500 homes make up the Pinecraft area. Since many Amish come for only a few weeks at a time, precise numbers of visitors are difficult to gauge.

While the atmosphere is relaxed, Amish people still adhere to the main church rules. Three-wheeled bicycles provide the most popular mode of transportation here, since buggies aren't practical or permitted on the streets of Sarasota. On a recent Sunday morning, a tiny corner lot was packed with bicycles. Inside the house, an Old Order Amish church service was in full swing. Gentle hymns could be heard riding a gentle balmy breeze.

Most residences here are tiny, equipped with just the bare basics. The occasional real estate auction attests to the stiff competition for obtaining some of the scarce lots.

A bit removed from the bustle of Pinecraft's main activity, tucked away on quiet Honore Street, there is even a school serving the area's Amish-Mennonite children. Following is a brief Q & A with the schoolmaster, Lester Gingerich:

QUESTION: Does Sunnyside enroll Anabaptist students from all orders?

GINGERICH: Yes, our school does enroll Old Order Amish, Beachy Amish, a couple other conservative Anabaptist affiliations, and Apostolic Christian.

QUESTION: What is Sunnyside's current enrollment?

GINGERICH: Our enrollment presently is about 52 which is a couple more than last year. We provide for Kindergarten through 12th grade. We use conventional class room setting for the younger grades and ACE individualized offices for grades 4 through high school.

QUESTION: Do you have many "transient" students - Amish children who are down in Sarasota for maybe just a few weeks or a month or so while wintering with their families?

GINGERICH: It has been more common in past years that visitors or Amish tourists in the winter send their children to our school, but the last several years not so. It depends largely if we have the capacity to handle them or are too full as is.

QUESTION: Can you tell us a little about Sunnyside's history, and any other information of interest about the Pinecraft community?

GINGERICH: Sunnyside began as a church in 1968 with another conservative affiliation and switched to the Beachy order in 1970. Our school was started in 1971 and has continued to this day. Besides our Beachy-Amish school there are two other Mennonite schools in our community. The one is by a church in the Rosedale Conservative Conference and the other is by the Mennonite Church USA.

We are a little over two miles east of Pinecraft just north of Bahia Vista and along Honore Avenue. We used to be pretty much in the country but the city has pretty well encompassed us.

While surrounding Sarasota continues to grow, Todd Emrich, doesn't think it'll ever get out of hand.

"Because of zoning it would be impossible for this to become a very touristy place, growth is so controlled here," Emrich says.

There is, by the way, a small enclave in Arizona, where Amish from Rexford, Montana, Kansas, and Colorado spend the winters...perhaps that place should be called "Pinecraft West."

EDITOR'S FAVORITE: FOUNTAIN CITY, INDIANA

The Amish settlements in Wayne County, Indiana are relatively new. Wayne County's largest city is Richmond, which was once home to a sprawling school bus factory. The school buses are long gone, and the area is now a sleepy agricultural outpost. It used to be that the nearest Amish were 60 miles to the north. Not anymore. Lured by plentiful farmland and roads free from gawking tourists, dozens of Amish families from Lancaster, Pennsylvania have moved to Wayne County in recent years.

Enough Amish families have come to Wayne County to create four new church districts. Several small businesses run by the Amish have been established. Fountain Acre Foods is one of the best. It's not the size of the place, it's really rather small. The store, though, is run like a well-oiled machine by husband and wife team, Stevie and Marianne Miller. The store is powered by gasoline appliances and the Miller's firm faith in a Higher Power. Fountain Acre Foods is part deli, part bakery, and part bulk food store. The feature an amazing array of spices, sugars, homemade noodles, and candies. The selection is just so diverse, from traditional to more offbeat. The store is located on Route 27 about 8 miles north of Richmond just outside the sleepy town of Fountain City, near Indiana's highest point. If you stop by Fountain Acres, tell Stevie and Marianne that The Amish Cook's editor sent you!

By the way, Fountain Acre Foods holds an annual cheese sale each April. Prices are outstanding. Here is a sampler:

Large horns of colby cheese: regularly $3.38 per pound. Sale price: $1.82 per pound.

Sliced yellow American: regularly $2.30 per pound. Sale price: $1.89 per pound.

2 pound roll of butter: $6.49. Sale price: $4.78.

THE AMISH OF MAINE

While visiting Smyrna, you will no doubt hear the clippity clop of horses trotting down the road. In 1996, a group of Amish families settled in Smyrna. This is a unique community settlement within a community. To drive through this section of town is like stepping into the pages of history. The families living in this settlement do not use electricity, or modern equipment. Horses are used for work and for travel. A horse drawn buggy full of children or a horse drawn wagon full of hay or lumber is a common site in Smyrna and the surrounding area.

The people are hardworking, industrious – creating several profitable businesses in Smyrna during economic challenging times. The business include, but are not limited to: Metal Shop - metal roofing and metal buildings, Sturdi Built – wooden buildings that can be used for camps, barns or storage sheds, Merri Gold Greenhouse, a leather goods and harness shop, a furniture shop, a bicycle repair shop and a general store. The general store is a joy to visit. The store has everything an old time general store would have – gum, canning jars, cast iron fry pans, books, bolts, food, and lanterns to name a few items.

While keeping in their own community for school and church – the people are neighborly, friendly, hardworking, and honest. The children are polite, well mannered and friendly. This growing community is a beehive of activity during the day and they welcome the public to visit their businesses and share in their church meetings.

KENT COUNTY, DELAWARE

Each Amish settlement interacts with its non-Amish neighbors in different ways, sometimes positively, sometimes negatively, sometimes neutrally. In Kent County, Delaware buggy safety has been a top priority among the non-Amish. In Kent County the Amish community creates unique situations for the motoring public. Amish buggies are horse-drawn vehicles that travel at less than 10 mph. It is very easy to come upon one quickly, with little time to react.

The Kent County Traffic Safety Committee has addressed this issue in a variety of ways. The committee has provided amber flashing lights to the Amish community, as well as reflective leg bands for the horses to wear. These efforts will increase buggy visibility at night and in low-light situations. In addition, a brochure detailing safety concerns for the motoring public has been developed and will be available in the Division of Motor Vehicle lanes, as well as in Delaware's tourism and travel offices. Finally, new signage has been created. These signs will be placed on roadways where the Amish frequently travel, in an effort to alert motorists to use caution where there is a greater likelihood of sharing the road with a horse-drawn vehicle.

AMISH "GHOST TOWN"

Trenton, Ohio is a small, relatively non-descript suburban town orbiting 30 miles north of sprawling Cincinnati, Trenton is home to tidy vinyl-sided subdivisions and the giant MillerCoors brewery, which supplies much of the Midwest with beer. I spent most of the 1990s writing about Trenton and the surrounding farmlands for the local newspaper, covering craft shows, sports teams, and business openings. Just to the south of Trenton, nestled in a quiet bend in the Great Miami River is a ghost wisp of a town known as Woodsdale. Woodsdale today consists of a few homes and a business or two. But Woodsdale wasn't always so sleepy. It was once home to a thriving riverside amusement park which was the Kings Island or Six Flags of its day. Called "Woodsdale Island Park," the venue featured rides and entertainment and catered to well-heeled Cincinnatians who would take the train to the park for the day. The park began a slow decline around the turn-of-the-century and was dealt a death blow by 1913's ravaging floods, from which it never recovered. But it is the time before Woodsdale's amusement park glory days that the Amish tilled the land, and traces of this past are preserved for future generations to enjoy at the Chrisholm Historic Farmstead. Chrisholm is the home of Samuel Augspurger, one of the leaders of the Amish settlement at the time. The home was built in 1874. Other homes in the Woodsdale area also remain that were part of this once vibrant Amish settlement. Disagreements and changes ultimately let to the settlement's disbanding in the 1800s, but the nearby Trenton Mennonite Church congregation which worships today just a few miles away is a remnant of the 1800s Amish community.

Miller Brewing Company plant spews steam and the rumble of beer trucks punctuates the quiet afternoons. The suburban sprawl of Cincinnati has spread all around Woodsdale, but prosperity seems to have passed this burg by. As noted, things weren't always so bleak, though, in this tiny outpost. Turn of the 20th century Woodsdale boasted a hotel, railroad depot, post office, saloons and the nearby amusement park.

Before the park turned Woodsdale into a local tourist attraction, it was the site of one of Ohio's first Amish settlement. Christian Augspurger and his family were Old Order Amish. They were lured to the area by inexpensive and plentiful farmland. The first Augspurgers arrived in 1829 and were soon followed by a number of Amish families, some closely connected to Jacob Amman, the founder of the church. Ropp was a prominent early name in the church and records show several family members lived in the Woodsdale community briefly in the 1830s before settling in Illinois. Eicher, another common Amish name, were among the names of settlers also. The Butler County Amish farms were well-kept and tidy. The settlement, though, never really grew beyond several dozen families and there were divisions along theological and philosophical lines. By the late 1800s most of the Amish families had moved to central Illinois where the communities of Arthur and Arcola thrive to this day. The remaining Amish in the area assimilated into the surrounding population, their German dialect becoming lost to time. If one looks closely, there are still signs of the original Amish presence in the area around Trenton, Ohio. A sturdy two-story white brick structure in downtown Trenton bears the faded name: "The Eicher Building." The Trenton Mennonite Church is among the few Mennonite congregations for hundreds of miles. This church was started by the descendants of the area's original Amish settlers. Men sat on side on the church and women the other – as is Amish custom – until well into the 1900s. And the centerpiece of preservation for Butler County's Amish settlement is now part of the area Metroparks system. The park is called Chrisholm, which features the well-preserved original farmstead of Christian and Samuel Augspurger.

OTHER AMISH "GHOST TOWNS"

A new Amish settlement needs several ingredients for success: plenty of available land, a welcoming ideology, and jobs, whether they be farming or factory. But more often than not ideological differences doom a settlement. Sometimes an ideological divide will get so bad, will so poison the atmosphere that everyone just picks up and leaves. Consider this email from a reader:

"Do you have any idea what happened to the Amish community in Rosebush, Michigan? I have visited their bakery for years...and it is closed and most of the Amish have left the area. It was like they left without anyone even noticing..."

Rosebush, Michigan and a similar settlement in the town of Ovid seemingly vanished overnight, their residents dispersing to Amish communities near and far.

AMISH LANGUAGE: FACT & FICTION

What is Amish language?

The Amish language is analogous to Cajun French in Louisiana several generations ago (the language really isn't commonly spoken anymore, except as novelty and by some very old-timers). Cajun French, like Amish German, morphed from its mother tongue into an almost unrecognizable gumbo of English, Creole, and French by the mid-20th century. If a Parisian were to find a fluent speaker of Cajun French deep in a bayou somewhere today, they would probably have a very difficult time conversing. Amish dialects of German have also evolved to the point that someone from Bavaria could probably converse with a Pennsylvania Dutch person in the United States, but it would likely be a halting dialogue with difficultly understanding. Amish German has become infused with English words and has evolved far from its original language. Almost all Amish speak and understand English with little difficultly, although there is often a subtle, but noticeable, German accent or Swiss lilt in their voices. Most Amish write quite well in English, some do know written German grammar, but they rarely mix the two. Amish education is very well-grounded in bilingualism.

In works of popular fiction, you often have Amish people portrayed as speaking a somewhat different kind of English. But these are all simply "literary devices." Literary devices are common tools authors use to differentiate characters and make a read more entertaining. Reading a popular mass market Amish-themed fiction novel, for instance, where an Amish character says "Gut day, I'm goin' to go fishin' now" makes for fun reading and easily identifies a character as Amish. A novel about the Amish wouldn't provide as much of an escapist experience if the author wrote "Good day, I'm going to go fishing now." Literary devices are a fine, acceptable way for an author to make a point, but one always needs to know the difference so they can separate fact from fiction. But don't take it from me. Scan the pages of the Amish newspaper, The Budget. Hundreds and hundreds of letters from Amish authors across the country appear on its pages each week. I've never seen a letter from an Amish scribe that employs Beverly Lewis-type literary devices with folksy tidbits sprinkled in such as "Gut day", "What a blessin" or Jah. These are all fictional literary devices, again, perfectly acceptable in the world of make-believe but not terribly reflective of reality.

Chapter 2

AMISH COOK MEMORIES & THE EDITOR'S BOOKSHELF

TRIBUTE TO ELIZABETH COBLENTZ: THE ORIGINAL AMISH COOK

"I retire for the day, my mind is wondering will this letter be of interest to others?"

That humble question, the opening of Elizabeth's first column in August 1991, was the beginning of a literary legacy. I was 19 and Elizabeth was 55 and wise in the ways of her world. It was the start of journey we would begin together. And what indescribable sadness I felt that our journey came to such a sudden, unexpected ending last week with her death.

I came to her asking her to write a weekly newspaper column that I would edit and submit to newspapers, and she graciously, although maybe skeptically, agreed. We were an entrepreneurial odd couple. I don't think either of us ever expected that she would one day touch so many lives, and appear in over 100 newspapers.

Elizabeth gave me enough memories and life lessons to carry me through the rest of my years. I think of warm summer afternoons, and the sun nourishing Elizabeth's bountiful garden. I think of the tangy smell of fresh rhubarb pie rising from her oven. I think of our quiet chats; my first taste of oatmeal pie; her steaming one-kettle soup; clothes on the line, flapping in the wind; of Elizabeth and Ben sitting around the supper table, their love for one another obvious. I remember Elizabeth at her kitchen table, tenderly transforming a rough pile of picked dandelions into a soothing salad. She always said a dandelion salad for supper would make for a relaxing night's sleep. I think of Elizabeth with her grandchildren, patiently nurturing them from infancy to adolescence. I think of her amazing and equal love for all eight of her wonderful children, who are now all adults.

Whenever I would visit Elizabeth, even long after the novelty should have worn off, I would feel a sense of tranquility come over me. It was as if Elizabeth's home were my shelter, a place that shielded me from our increasingly difficult to understand world. I think her column provided readers with that same sense of shelter.

Perhaps one of my most cherished moments with Elizabeth came this past spring. I was staying at her house for a few days while a photographer was in town taking photos of Elizabeth's farm for her new book. I didn't want to feel like a freeloader, so I told Elizabeth I would earn my stay by tending to her garden. I spent almost two full days in the garden, pulling weeds and clearing ground. I'm someone accustomed to tapping computer keys, not yanking thistles out of the soil. But the warm spring sun felt good and by the second day I had learned the best way to grab a thistle and yank it out by the roots. Once, Elizabeth joined me in the garden with her hoe. She seemed to glide across the soft earth, effortlessly tending to her young sprouts. We talked a little. But mostly we just silently worked, bonding in the satisfaction of work well done. Occasionally, she would break into song, as she often did while gardening. It was a haunting Swiss medley, passed down through generations, from another time and place. Elizabeth was a living link to a more tranquil era, a time when self-sufficiency and family were the medals of a life well lived.

While Elizabeth lived a simple life, she was not a simple woman. Elizabeth cherished her privacy, but enjoyed her celebrity. During the few public appearances she made, she worked the crowd like a seasoned author. Yet when the last book had been signed, she would always remark: "I feel so unworthy of the attention." Elizabeth had an ornery and humorous streak, always ribbing me about my girlfriends and messy car. Elizabeth had little formal education, but she was street-wise. Or in her world, gravel-road wise. As I sometimes clumsily navigated my way into adulthood, Elizabeth patiently waited. To her, life was like one of the colorful quilts she spent so much time creating: lots of labor, many mistakes, but in the end, if one tried hard enough, the journey would create an end worthy of admiration.

"In so many ways we should be thankful. But maybe too often we forget"; Elizabeth wrote in an early column. Elizabeth was always reminding us not to forget life's simple pleasures: the song of a bird, the smile of a grandchild, the smell of fresh laundry, warm popcorn on a cold winter's night.

It all ended last week when Elizabeth succumbed, the victim of an aneurysm, before a book-signing in Independence, Missouri. As I stood by her bedside during her final moments in a Missouri hospital, I thought back to the first time I pulled into the Coblentz driveway and those warm wonderful memories, and I grieved that the journey had ended. But through tears, I know that in some small way, our journey will continue: Elizabeth's words remain, motivating us all to seek and savor simplicity.

I think with time, she learned the answer to the question she so innocently asked in her first column: Yes, Elizabeth, your letters were of great interest to others.

AN AMISH CHRISTMAS

FROM THE EDITOR'S DESK

While the rest of us are now caught up in a chaotic carnival of shopping, light-stringing, and holiday party preparation, there's a portion of our population that seems unfazed by the season.

Christmas in the Amish community isn't the materialistic affair that it is in the rest of the country. Walk into most Amish homes and you won't see a Christmas tree, no lights, no wreaths, no pine-scented garland strung above the mantle. Adhering to their bedrock beliefs to following a simple sacrament, the Amish keep Christmas "plain." The only hint in Elizabeth's home that the holiday is near are the colorful Christmas cards sent by well-wishers which she keeps on a shelf above one of her rocking chairs in the living room.

That's not to say that the Amish don't mark Christmas. Indeed, there are gifts to buy and presents to wrap, but it's all a much more low-key event.

On a recent visit to Elizabeth's, she was lamenting about what gifts to get for her over 30 grandchildren. That dilemma pales in comparison to what her grandparents must have faced every Christmas: getting gifts for over 100 grandchildren. Once again, though, simplicity saves the day. Elizabeth's grandparents would give each of their 100 grandchildren a small plastic bag filled with colorful candy. Also in each bag would be a small dish or handkerchief. These small tokens have become priceless treasures over time as the grandchildren grew into adults. Elizabeth is contemplating something similar for her own brood of grandchildren.

And, of course, there's holiday baking which wins out over shopping in most Amish homes. You'll find few fancy fruitcakes or flaming rum punches among the Pennsylvania Dutch. The food served during holiday gatherings is simple, but with a hint of elegance. Most families have one big gathering during the season. For Elizabeth and her family, that day has always been New Year's Day.

The children will arrive at dawn in their horse-drawn buggies for a full-course breakfast: perhaps a ham and cheese casserole, home-baked cinnamon rolls, and Elizabeth's home-made biscuits and gravy. Additional folding tables are set up in Elizabeth's dining room to accommodate her whole family at once. A noon lunch and dinner will be served with sauerkraut, homemade stew, and from-scratch bread. Lots of singing and yodeling takes place during the day, and the grandchildren add energy and love to the occasion.

In some ways, the Amish way of celebrating Christmas makes much more sense.

FINAL DAY ON THE COBLENTZ FARM

By Kevin Williams

Most of me didn't want to go to the auction. So it was with a sense of dread and duty that I pulled myself out of bed early on Saturday, June 14, to attend the estate auction of Elizabeth Coblentz. There were many reasons I didn't want to attend, not the least of which was that I didn't exactly have a wad of money itching to be spent at an auction. But there were other reasons: Part of me didn't want to go simply because it was yet another sad reminder of Elizabeth's passing. Another part of me was mystified by their tradition of auctioning off all the deceased's belongings to the highest bidder. In this Amish area of Indiana, it's just the way things are done, my girlfriend, Rachel, kept reminding me. The estate auction is as much a part of Amish culture as a will and testament is of mine.

Amish auctions are typically a low-key event. They're attended mainly by area Amish (after all, how many of us need kerosene lamps and horse harnesses?) and a handful of non-Amish locals. Obviously, Elizabeth's reach was much wider, and that made me uneasy. The Amish believe in equality among themselves, I didn't want other local Amish resentful of Elizabeth's family if too many outsiders attended.

Personally, I dreaded the thought of having a legion of readers of The Amish Cook column descending upon Elizabeth's property. To me, Elizabeth's home is hallowed ground. My relationship with readers has always been paradoxical. I love the readers, the readers whose warmth, kindness, and selflessness through cards and correspondence kept Elizabeth motivated to write "The Amish Cook" all those years. But Elizabeth's family is like family to me, and I've grown fiercely protective of them. After all, Elizabeth never sought celebrity. When I pulled into her driveway so many years ago, I pledged to her that the column would never take away her cherished privacy. So the thought of readers coming to Elizabeth's home disturbed me. But there the sign was in her front yard: PUBLIC AUCTION. This meant, in the great tradition of Amish auctions, everyone was welcome. So I put aside my mixed emotions and arrived at Elizabeth's.

An ocean of automobiles was outnumbered only by a passel of horse and buggies. Chestnut colored equines grazed gently in the lazy little woods next to Elizabeth's large two-story house.

I had never attended a public auction before, and after a two-hour drive I was tired. But I quickly learned that one must not stretch at an auction, because I found the auctioneer accepting my unintentional $120 bid for a corn sheller. Luckily someone else wanted the corn-sheller more than I and let me off the hook.

I really came to get one of Elizabeth's rocking chairs. It's a chair that she and her husband, Ben, had sat in numerous times, gently rocking by the warmth of a coal-stove fire. Bidding quickly commenced on the rockers, and my efforts were rewarded with a win. I'll treasure this wooden rocker. The Amish are not, as a rule, very

materialistic, so even the most seemingly sentimental items are put on the auction block.

The farmhouse itself was put up for sale. For a tense hour two bidders (anonymous at the time) submitted competing bids. I had hoped the property would stay in Elizabeth's family, and they tried, ultimately unsuccessfully. But our second hope was that the farm would remain in Amish hands. And it did. A local farmer purchased the 104 acre parcel, which adjoins his. Perhaps one of his children will take the farmhouse and it will remain in Amish hands for generations more to come.

As the auctioneer chattered away prices and bids, I soaked in the sights and sounds, and I was pleased with what I saw. There were some readers at the event, but for the most part it was a traditional Amish auction. About 80 percent of those in attendance were Amish. Amish women bid on prized pots and pans, safe from us for another generation. Bearded, bespectacled Amish men stood by the wooden split-rail fence and chatted about farm equipment and crops. I was watching a tradition of generations unfold. Us non-Amish seemed to settle into an easy rapport with our Amish hosts. It was, as all Amish auctions are, a coming together of two cultures, a touching of two worlds.

Laundry lines that once groaned under the weight of freshly washed clothes swung empty in the wind. The barn which once housed so many milk cows stared vacantly at rolling fields barely untouched by time. At the end of the day, horse-drawn buggies clattered along gravel roads to their warm family-filled homes.

The auction was not what I had originally feared it would be. It was orderly, poignant, and mainly Amish. As Rachel and I left that day, saying our goodbyes to Susan and Verena and Lovina's children, I felt like Elizabeth was looking down upon us that day. And if she was, I am sure she was smiling.

Meanwhile, almost a full 10 years after bidding on that rocker, it sits in my living room, a gentle reminder of a gentle woman.

OTHER FAVORITE MEMORIES:

These are some favorite editor's memories from the days when Elizabeth Coblentz wrote the column from her Indiana farm....

- Homemade rhubarb jam at Elizabeth Coblentz's
- Taking Ben Coblentz into town to buy huge blocks of ice for the ice chest
- Sleep-overs by the cozy coal-stove
- Unruly rhubarb patch unfurling each spring
- Ripe autumn apples from the Amish Cook's mini apple-orchard
- Milking time in the barn.....
- The smell of homemade cinnamon rolls rising in the oven....
- Elizabeth Coblentz's hearty laugh....
- Talking baseball with Ben Coblentz....
- Billowing loaves of homemade bread.....
- Relaxing in the living room rocking chairs....
- Homemade sandwich spread....
- Fresh cucumbers from the garden....
- A heavy, wet snowfall bringing out the horse-drawn sleighs..

BOOK SHELF

There are a ton of great books out there about the Amish (and some really bad ones, too!). A good, indepth book rich in detail and perspective can be a wonderful way to learn about the enigmatic Amish. Here are my top picks, some are classics in the Anabaptist community, others more obscure:

A HISTORY OF THE AMISH, BY STEPHEN NOLT: this is the first book about the Amish that ever read. I think it holds up well over time and provides an excellent primer about the Amish.

AMISH GRACE: HOW FORGIVENESS TRASCENDED TRAGEDY by Stephen Nolt, Donald Kraybill, and David Weaver. This is a more recent read, a superb book about Amish forgiveness in the context of the tragic Pennsylvania school shooting.

PLAIN SECRETS: AN OUTSIDER AMONG THE AMISH by Joe MacKall. An excellent, easy read about one man's relationship with his Swartzentruber Amish neighbors.

Amish Peace: Simple Wisdom for a Complicated World by Fisher, Suzanne Woods

Chapter 3

AMISH IN THE NEWS
NEWS & COMMENTARY FROM THE
AMISH COOK'S EDITOR

What Were They Thinking?

Duh.....

An astute entrepreneur probably wouldn't open a scuba diving school in North Dakota or vegetarian restaurant among the stockyards of Kansas City, so why was the Ohio government pushing food stamps on the Amish? The Amish reject almost all forms of insurance and government assistance.

In 2006, The Ohio Office of Family Stability began demanding that local welfare workers somehow get Amish people to sign up for food stamps. The reasoning was that most Amish would be eligible on the basis of income. However, when caseworkers began arriving at Amish homes to sell them on the idea, they were met with blank stares and shut doors. One caseworker left with two loaves of homemade bread, not exactly a sign of a "hungry" family. By refusing to sign up, the Amish were lowering the local food stamp participation rates which, apparently, made the agency look bad in the eyes of government bean-counters. Once the story hit the newspapers, though, the agency became a laughingstock.

How about some supper instead?

Okay, I'm not minimizing a home-invasion. Normally a home-invasion would be scary, but this sounds borderline humorous. A young man not much larger than a featherweight boxer shows up at an Amish home in Nappanee, Indiana in 2010 and demands - get this - $20. What idiot puts on a ski mask, enters an unlocked home, brandishes a knife, and risks going to prison for *twenty dollars*??? He's lucky the Amish are pacifists because the robber, being only 5'2, would probably have been beaten to a pulp by anyone else. The Amish occupants said they didn't have any money on them, but they did offer him food. The would-be robber -upset that there wasn't any money - slashed the screen door and stormed away. The would-be robber really missed out! Amish suppers are the best you'll ever eat, If I were the robber I would have happily forgotten the $20 and taken them up on the food offer!

UM....Did You REALLY Think You Could Outrun the Cops?

LITTLE VALLEY, NEW YORK—The driver of a horse and buggy led Cattaraugus County sheriff's deputies on a three-mile pursuit through fields and woods early Monday morning, eventually abandoning the buggy and fleeing on foot.

It happened on Frank Road in Napoli, where deputies were investigating underage drinking.

Deputies reported they tried to stop the driver of the horse and buggy, but he drove the rig through fields and into the woods before jumping down and taking off on foot.

After searching without success for the driver, deputies took the horse and buggy back to a nearby home, and a young man was taken into custody.

Jonas J. Hershberger, 20, of Frank Road, was charged with overdriving of animals, reckless endangerment and obstructing governmental administration. Following arraignment in Little Valley Town Court, he was sent to the county jail in lieu of $250 bail.

And, yet another.....

In a desperate attempt to elude state police, a wanted Lancaster County man startled an Amish couple by jumping into their horse- drawn buggy in Honey Brook, troopers said.

"Are you being chased by the police?" the buggy driver inquired.

"Yes," replied Joshua Adam McElyea, 22, of Wertztown Road. Narvon.

"Then you got to step out," the buggy operator told him, according to a trooper from the Embreeville barracks.

McElyea hopped out of the buggy and ran into a cornfield, police said.

The driver of a drywall truck witnessed the pursuit and helped police catch McElyea, said Lt. Brian Naylor, station commander of the Embreeville barracks in Chester County.

The truck driver picked up two troopers who were chasing McElyea on foot and drove them into the cornfield.

Other troopers followed on foot to a spot where they surrounded McElyea and took him into custody, Trooper Brian Barber said.

Police in several counties, including Lancaster, had been seeking McElyea on outstanding warrants for two years, an Embreeville spokesman said.

Late Wednesday morning, Embreeville Trooper Dwayne Winchester spotted McElyea driving on Route 322 from Lancaster County into Chester County.

When Winchester tried to stop McElyea in Honey Brook, the wanted man turned into the parking lot of a magistrate court, and then started fleeing on foot, police said.

McElyea ran through several residential neighborhoods and fields in the southwest end of Honey Brook. The buggy riders were traveling on Walnut Street in the borough when McElyea made his sudden appearance, police said.

One trooper dislocated a finger during the pursuit of McElyea, the Embreeville spokesman said. McElyea complained of a headache and asthma attack after he was captured and was taken to Brandywine Hospital to be checked.

After being treated and released, McElyea was committed to Chester County Prison in default of $25,000 cash bail, police said.

McElyea faced charges of fleeing-eluding police and resisting arrest from the chase. Lancaster County authorities were seeking him for probation violation. He also was wanted for theft-by-deception and criminal mischief in Chester County, and for burglary and simple assault in Berks County, the Embreeville spokesman said.

BUGGY HIJACKINGS?

You would think hijacking a buggy would be fairly uncommon and, frankly, difficult. Yes, horse-drawn buggies do move much slowly than cars. But have any of you ever tried to climb into a moving buggy? And who would want to assault and terrify the pacifist occupants of a buggy? None of this seemed to deter the perpetrators of a spate of buggy hijackings in the fall of 2007 and spring of 2008.

In the fall of 2007, Christopher Lewis of Rising Sun, Maryland terrorized buggies in Lancaster County. Armed with a baseball bat, Lewis hijacked a couple of buggies, terrified the occupants, and fled in a car driven by some teenage girls. The boy's mother, at the sentencing of her son - who a jury found guilty - told the judge her son was "just trying to impress the girls." Sheesh, whatever happened to souping up one's car or joining the school's football team? True to their pacifist and forgiving nature, the Amish victims showed up at court asking for leniency and mercy.

And Another......

Some genius in Jamesport, Missouri decided he would try an armed hijacking of a buggy also in the spring of 2008. An armed robber commandeered an Amish buggy at gunpoint and ordered the driver to take him to a nearby trailer park to hide. In addition to scaring the daylights out of the Amish driver, plenty of witnesses saw the robber jump into the buggy which wasn't exactly the fastest getaway. Police caught up to the buggy and the red-handed robber in a matter of minutes.

THOSE ICED OVER ENGLISH!

MAYFIELD, Ky. - When the wind died down and the ice storm had passed, Joe Stutzman gathered his spare lanterns and stepped out of his Amish farmhouse to lend them to his modern-living neighbors.

"I feel sorry for my neighbors who were used to electricity and all of a sudden didn't have it," Stutzman said. "I know that must be hard for them."

Hundreds of thousands of people in Kentucky have been without electricity for their lights, furnaces, ovens and refrigerators since the killer storm hit more than a week ago, and some spots might not get power back for weeks.

Amish Politics

Indiana's dopey new law requiring photo ID to vote (never mind that there has not been one prosecuted case of voter fraud in the Hoosier State in recent history) prevented a handful of elderly nuns from voting in Indiana. Yes, you ALWAYS want to keep those nuns from voting, quite a lawless group (insert sarcastic tone). Meanwhile, WNDU TV in South Bend presented a story with the headline "Amish Turn Out To Vote in Election." Unless I am missing something the reporter went to a Chelsea Clinton Cinco de Mayo rally and found an articulate Amish man there who expressed support for the Clintons. Somehow I don't think finding one Amish person at a Chelsea Clinton rally should merit a headline "Amish Turn Out to Vote in Election." SIGH. I get exasperated with the media at times. My guess is that very, very few Amish participated yesterday.

Uninvited Neighbors

Now this is an interesting story out of Pennsylvania. A group of Amish people who had been shunned from the church were found inside the home of an Amish neighbor. The shunned family said they were just trying to see wedding decorations in the house since they were not invited to the event. This story is strange on many levels. First and foremost, though, it's strange that this event ever made it to the courts. I'm wondering if this is a fluke or illustrative of a trend by the Amish to involve law-enforcement more and more in their lives. This type of dispute would almost always be handled "internally." But I guess the trespassed people felt violated or threatened enough to call the cops. Strange. The family was, by the way, found guilty of criminal trespass and fined.

Speaking of neighbors...

A group of Pennsylvanians have been complaining for the past year about the noise created by a nearby Amish-run sawmill. A court found in favor of the neighbors and put restrictions on the hours of operation of the sawmill, but neighbors are now saying that is not enough. SIGH, sometimes, I guess, moving to the country isn't all it is cracked up to be. Still, someday, some how, Rachel and I would love to move out of the city and get some land to live on. Rachel's mother lives on 10 acres and just having that extra bit of breathing room really makes her place pleasant. We live on a postage-stamp sized parcel of land in the city. Recently Rachel and I finally decided to tackle a row of horrid looking honeysuckle bushes that lined our backyard. We used a chainsaw, clippers, and lots of muscle to remove about 10 of these monsters and replaced them with a 6-foot privacy fence. Now our dogs don't bark at every passer by and it's a 100 percent improvement aesthetically over the bushes - or so we thought. One of our neighbors, anonymously, filed a complaint with the city that the fence "blocks their view." Blocks their view of what? Our crappy-looking backyard? And the 10 foot high honeysuckles DIDN'T block their view?? So now the local city zoning board is involved and we have to fill out all this paperwork, go before the zoning board and all sorts of other bureaucratic hoops that I just get the idea don't exist as much out in rural areas....unless ,of course, you run a sawmill....

PERHAPS TRY LANCASTER COUNTY OR SHIPSHEWANA INSTEAD.....

I don't think you'll find many colorful brochures touting the Bergholz, Ohio Amish community as a place to go for buggy rides and family-style suppers. Let me give you some background first:

The Amish church is one of the most "decentralized" churches you'll find anywhere. What do I mean? Let's take the Roman Catholic church or the Latter Day Saints (Mormons). These two faiths are on the opposite end of the spectrum from the Amish, both these churches have one central seat of authority (Rome for the Catholics, Salt Lake for the Mormons). Centralized churches have clear chains of command, rules, and ways. You can attend a Catholic service in Tacoma, Washington or Nags Head, North Carolina and basically get the same service. Of course, there are many churches throughout the spectrum of centralization. The Amish church has no "central office" where rules are made and doctrines are developed. The seat of authority with each church rests with the local bishop. While most Amish churches hew to a pacifist doctrine, the lack of centralization can lead to splinter groups, renegade sects, and wayward congregations. Of course splinter groups occur in all churches but the Amish church seems to experience more splits and splinters than others. All of this leads me to Bergholz where local bishop Sam Mullet appears to rule with an iron fist. The atmosphere in this rural Ohio church district (west of Wheeling, WV) became so poisoned in late 2007 that it led to a stand-off with a local SWAT team. Violent threats were made against the sheriff.

One Bergholz resident reported:

This particular Amish church district is indeed a cult. Many of the families have fled in fear. The bishop is a tyrant, and reminds me very much of Jim Jones and the Guyana Tragedy. The Sheriff went to that school house with ONE deputy to start. Wilma Troyer scared the children and told them the sheriff would hurt them. She then gathered the children around her and slowly walked back to the farmhouse where she took all the children inside. This is when the Sheriff called for backup, to protect himself and the deputy AND the other children. The Troyer children NEEDED to be removed, and I sincerely wish the rest of the children were removed, before they are all scared both emotionally and physically. Those not familiar with the situation have NO idea what is going on there. I was very close with many of the families who left, and am aware of the abuse this Mullet man has inflicted on his church members. Pray for the innocents still imprisoned there (Mullet will not let anyone else leave).

I've received correspondence from people in that community that claim that Mullet's Amish community is ruled by fear and is different from other Amish settlements. So, if you are looking for a nice, peaceful touristy Amish experience...um..stay away from Bergholz.

UH...IS THIS MAN AMISH?

This is a strange story on several levels. Here's the gist: a Lancaster County man - who claims he is Amish - was taken to court for making suspicious financial transactions. First of all, in the stringent post 9-11 environment banks routinely report to the Feds cash deposits and withdrawals from bank accounts that are $10,000 or more in a single day. These reports are called SARS (Suspicious Activity Reports). Of course, for people who have money and don't want to draw the ire of the Feds, they'll just make sure they avoid the $10,000 threshold by depositing $9500 or $9800.

This avoidance has created a crime called "structuring." So the government creates the $10,000 level, but then also creates the crime of "structuring" to avoid the $10,000. In perhaps the most famous example of SARS tripping someone up, New York Governor Elliot Spitzer was brought down by these SARS. His $9000 deposits were to fund his trysts with call girls. Which brings us to the Lancaster County man, Levi Stoltzfoos.

First of all, Stoltzfoos claims he is Amish but the Feds dispute that. This really is irrelevant other than Stoltzfoos's attorney claiming that the Amish routinely make large cash deposits. I have to say that maybe some Amish people have that kind of money, but I doubt that Amish people routinely walk around with $10,000 cash on them. The investigators apparently acted like the Keystone Cops, which I think undermines their case. But perhaps what has me scratching my head is that, in the end, no one is ever saying Stoltzfoos did anything illegal with the money. The only thing he ever did was make deposits and withdrawals under $10,000. At least Spitzer transported a prostitute across state lines. This whole case is just bizarre and probably a waste of taxpayer money.

NOT QUITE ROMEO AND JULIET

Lakeview - Michigan State Police say a 15-year-old Amish girl from Montcalm County was recovered at the Mexican border, and will be reunited with her family.

Investigators say Esther Herschberger left her family's home near Coral on February 24th. They say the girl left a note in her room telling her parents they should not worry.

Police say Esther called family friends on February 28th, asking them to tell her parents she was okay and in New York State. The next day, the friends received another call from someone crying. They believed the caller was Esther, but they were disconnected before anyone spoke.

Michigan State Police say they determined Esther was actually in Chicago when the call was made. They found out Esther travelled south to Mexico, where Mexican authorities detained her as she attempted to enter the country.

Police say the girl was in the company of 33-year-old Osvaldo Jaimes, a man from the Cedar Springs area. When investigators questioned Esther, she told them she planned to go to Mexico to marry James.

Police have made arrangements to reunite Esther with her family in Laredo, Texas, within the next 24 hours.

AUGUST 22, 2002 - MARTINSBURG, OHIO

An Amish couple said they will not compromise their religious beliefs and update an outhouse on their land, despite a judge's deadline.

Dan and Lena Miller said they would rather go to jail than install a watertight, concrete tank under the new outhouse they built for their son, who lives with his wife on an adjacent farm. A Knox County judge ruled last week that they must make the $200 update by Sept. 16.

The outhouse is next to a stream, creating the health risk that human waste can leak into the area's water supply, Health Commissioner Dennis Murray said.

The Millers have resisted complying with county law for nearly two years, he said.

The Millers use decomposed waste from the outhouse to fertilize wheat, barley, corn and oats on their farm in Clay Township, about 40 miles northeast of Columbus. Health workers first tried to convince the Millers to make the changes on their own, Murray said.

"We really didn't want to go to court," he said. "They are peaceful people, and they want to be left alone, but they need to have something that protects our groundwater just like everyone else."

The Millers, who have not attended court hearings, said they are exempt for religious reasons from county building codes. The couple belongs to the Swartzentrubers, a conservative group of Old Order Amish. The Christian denomination shuns modern conveniences such as electricity and indoor plumbing.

Many Amish also drink from contaminated, rusty drinking wells, said Jim Hoorman, a water quality agent for the Ohio State University Extension Service. More than half the wells he's tested in Hardin and Logan counties have unhealthy bacteria levels, contaminated by barnyard waste and outhouse seepage.

Bishop Dan Slabaugh, who leads the community of 150 in Clay Township, said almost everyone does things the same way as the Millers.

"If we go over our lifestyle and don't pay attention to it, things will go fast to an end," Slabaugh said. "We should keep with what we was taught."

An Ashland County Amish man spent several days in jail in the 1990s after citing religious reasons for refusing a Health Department request to bring his outhouse up to code.

County officials eventually persuaded the local bishop to approve an alternative septic system, similar to the concrete container the Millers must install.

Knox County is willing to give the Millers another chance, assistant prosecutor Ana Aebi said.

"We're going to make an extraordinary effort to make sure they understand what's needed," Aebi said. "But if we do not hear from them by Sept. 16, the judge will issue an order to arrest them."

AMISH MARKETING

WIEN, WISCONSIN - Even though Moses Troyer doesn't have a phone, a car, a computer or electricity, he still manages to market his small business.

But it isn't easy.

The Amish man and his family - wife Katie, sons Mose Junior and Joe, and daughter Rebecca - recently opened Troyer's Rugs, a small shop that sells hand-woven and crocheted rugs, place mats, handbags and chair pads at W370 Highway N.

A roadside sign, word-of-mouth and simple brochures make up the bulk of the Troyer marketing efforts. But there are times when Troyer will hitch a horse to a buggy and make the 11Ú2-mile trek into Edgar to use a pay phone to talk with customers or give a call to a newspaper to generate free publicity.

The family is part of what Troyer describes as a growing segment of the Amish population that relies on small business efforts and craftsmanship rather than traditional farming to earn a living. It means negotiating and dealing with the outside world more than ever, and it also means making decisions about how and when to use modern methods to let people know about their products.

"It has a tendency to make a more liberal group," Troyer said.

The Amish people will use modern conveniences, such as the phone, and will ride in cars driven by other people, he said, but they won't own those items.

They are always behind the rest of society. "It's our way to be second and be contented," Troyer said. "But it does make it a little more difficult."

The location of the business itself is an effort to market it. The family lived and worked in rural Taylor County, on a lightly traveled road. Troyer researched the Highway N property, and says 80 vehicles pass by each day. He thinks that drop-in traffic will spur sales.

"I anticipate it's going to boost my business, maybe double it," he said.

He also hired a printing shop to create a brochure that advertises his products, and he puts those brochures in areas where he thinks tourists and other people congregate.

Troyer has called newspapers in the hope of getting stories done. When a weekly Medford paper did a story on the business in 1998, it gave his business an upswing that lasted until he moved last May.

He doesn't use the word "Amish" in his marketing effort. The use of his faith and religion to sell a product doesn't appeal to him, although other Amish businessmen do it. "I want the product to stand on its own," he said.

He does, however, have a horse and buggy on his flier, and touts the fact the rugs are "like Grandma made."

Troyer is on the right marketing track, said Kirk Howard, president of the decidedly modern marketing firm of Kinzie & Green Inc. in Wausau.

Not using modern technology "is not something we actually faced" he said, but he says Troyer is doing a good job targeting his customers.

Moving the business was smart, he said. "The old adage is location, location, location."

He would recommend that Troyer find a way to get into craft shows or other types of sales, where customers are readily available.

Jim Elliott, an account executive with the firm, agrees, and said "Troyer's efforts at contacting newspapers is good, too & I would certainly attempt to do that publicity in other areas of the state, like the Milwaukee Journal. Who knows? They might like the story. It's unique."

MORE AMISH MARKETING....

I often receive press releases from Miller's Bakery and Furniture in Unity, Ohio. Miller's is a complex of businesses owned by an Amish family in the area and while they may not have the internet in keeping with their traditions, they are still able to harness its power.

The business works through a non-Amish (of course) PR firm that distributes information to media types like myself.

It's funny because the press release takes a "gentle dig" at its "rival" Holmes County, Ohio by starting out:

Northeast Ohio is known to have the largest Amish population in the world – so large and commercial now, Amish way of life is threatened. Over the past two generations, families have set out in search of more solitude creating a modern wagon train across Ohio and the country. Deep in the foothills of Southern Appalachia Ohio, the rural and traditional Amish way of life is preserved. The community is known as the Wheat Ridge Amish because of the long and winding country road that seems like a journey back in time to Nineteenth Century America.

As most of you know, I LOVE Adams County precisely because it is NOT too commercial and the Amish in Wheat Ridge recognize that....so they want to market that ambiance, but, of course, not TOO much because then it becomes Holmes County all over again. So it's a very delicate balance.

The press release continues:

Out on Wheat Ridge Road in West Union, Ohio the senses dance to the rhythmic spin of a buggy wheel, the harmony of a handcrafted armoire getting fine tuned, and the hypnotizing breeze that carries oven-fresh-baked apple pie across the field. It's a special place where time stands still and Sundays are still reserved for God.

Stop the world and enter Ohio's other Amish Country. The old saying, they don't make it like they used to, isn't even thinkable at Miller's Bakery, Furniture and Bulk Foods stores. There, not much has changed over the decades since Harry and Lydia Miller settled on a 300-acre farm in 1977. From the get-go, they introduced the surrounding countryside to their family's original baking recipes. Ma and Pa plus their six children used to line the porch of the farmhouse with goods straight out of the oven so they can cool. It wasn't long before they shared their fixings with curious neighbors. Then the secret was out.

Before the Miller family knew it, more and more people stopped by wanting to buy bread, pies, cinnamon roll, you name it. Eventually, even handmade furniture entered the mix. Harry would often visit Holmes County, Ohio and bring back furniture, which sold, well, like hotcakes. The more trips Harry made, the more furniture he sold. So, the farming days for the Miller's, raising cattle, hogs, sheep and such gave way to a thriving baking and woodworking business. As years and then decades past, the Millers kept expanding to meet the ever growing demand. Today, there are 34,000 square feet of furniture under one roof, plus more outside, and a separate building for the bakery and another for the bulk food store. The cash registers are powered by wind-generated energy. Plus the Miller's use a lot of solar energy and air compressors. In the parking lot, it's not uncommon for a horse and buggy to be standing next to a BMW.

And the rest of the press release is just pure marketing genius, the history, the special events, and it obviously works, because it got me to run it in its entirety! Here is the rest:

In its third generation, with a fourth learning the ropes, the thriving Amish merchants of Adams County, Ohio have regular visitors from Cincinnati, Columbus, Dayton, Portsmouth and Kentucky. They even meet mail-order demand from across the country and overseas. Most of Harry and Lydia's children run things now. Daniel is at the Furniture Store, Larry at the Bakery, and Harry Jr. at the Bulk Food Store. Malinda helps too. The other two sons, Gerold and David come back often to visit. All together, the six children have provided Harry and Lydia more than 20 grandchildren. With that, the family business and legacy looks like it will continue for many years to come.

Every year, the Miller's show their customer appreciation by offering special events and sales during Memorial Day Weekend, Labor Day Weekend, Fall Cookout, End of Year Clearance and from time-to-time, quilt auctions and other special occasions. Their 2010 calendar of offerings includes **(this calendar is for 2010, the same events are generally held each year according to Miller, obviously the days will be different)**

May 28, 29 and 31 of 2010: Memorial Day storewide sale (furniture store only, excluding outdoor building and gazebos). Ten percent off all items in stock and special orders placed during sales dates.

September 2, 3, 4 and 6: Labor Day sale (furniture store only, excluding outdoor building and gazebos). Ten percent off all items in stock and special order placed during sales dates.

September 4: Thirteenth Annual Amish School Benefit Cookout (hamburgers, hot dogs, chips, fresh pie, homemade ice cream, coffee and soft drinks.

September 24 school benefit auction

October 2 is the 33rd Annual Miller's Anniversary Customer Appreciation Day. Get your free 2011 calendar with our sale dates (BBQ chicken, baked beans, cole slaw, fresh pie, homemade ice cream, coffee and soft drinks).

November 26 & 27: Miller's Thanksgiving Sale (furniture store only, excluding outdoor building and gazebos). Ten percent off all items in stock and special order placed during sales dates.

December 27, 28, 29, 30, 31, 2010 and January 1, 2011: End of Year Clearance Sale. Ten percent off all items in stock at furniture store. Bakery *will have free coffee and cookies. Bulk Food Store will have free cheese and candy samples.*

Now, I have to put in my own plug, if you do visit Adams County, don't forget to also stop in at the Keim Family Market, an absolutely delightful place right off Route 32!

AMISH HEATERS?

During the frigid winter of 2009, newspapers and magazines across the United States carried ads with banner headlines screaming:
"Amish man's new miracle idea helps home heat bills hit rock bottom"

In reality, the devices were nothing more than a standard 1500 watt electric space heater. Most national chain stores were selling similar space heaters for 30 dollars. But those models weren't wrapped in an alleged Amish-made mantel. The advertisements shrill pitch emphasized that Amish craftsmen were "working their fingers to the bone" making the mantels. The reality was less glamorous: a handful of Amish from a liberal Ohio sect work in the factory where the mantels are made. There was a time when newspapers, as the caretakers of truth, probably would have turned away such an advertisement. But cash-starved dailies devoured the dollars pouring in from Heat Surge, the Canton, Ohio based manufacturer. TNS Media Intelligence, an advertising tracking firm, estimates the company spent $44.2 *million* dollars trying to sell $299 "Amish heaters" to the American public.

Their ubiquitous ads featured bearded, smiling Amish men standing by a toasty hearth touting the "miracle heater." Some full-page newspaper ads pictured an Amish husband and wife heading home with a couple of heaters strapped into the back of their buggy. Setting aside the pesky detail that the Old Order Amish don't use electricity or believe in miracles, the company sold a staggering numbers of these units. Perhaps the only real miracle is that so many people bought it.

MURDER IN AMISH COUNTRY

This incident in Holmes County, Ohio received amazingly little attention locally or nationally, but it was a fascinating - and tragic - case that unfolded during the summer of 2009.

A murder was the tragic outcome of a "love triangle" between Amish mother of five, Barbara Weaver, her husband Eli Weaver, and Barbara Raber. Raber, who is Mennonite, was having an affair with Eli - a jury later found - for *six years*. Weaver and Raber decided that they wanted to be together and the only impediment to that was Barbara. So Raber, in the pre-dawn hours on a warm summer day, sneaked into the Weaver home and shot Barbara to death while she slept. Eli was away fishing at the time but it was later proved at trial that he helped in planning his wife's murder. All of this occurred while the five Weaver children were home asleep. A jury later found Raber guilty and she was sentenced to 23 years in prison. Although Eli Weaver didn't pull the trigger, he was also found culpable for conspiracy and sent to the slammer.

Lets run-down the reasons why this story is so unusual:

1. Homicides in the Amish community are extraordinarily rare. The Nickel Mines school shooting several years ago was an anomaly. Murders of a domestic sort are even more rare. You could probably count the occurrences on your hands over the past century that they have occurred in the Amish community.

2. Adulterous affairs involving Amish are rare. This likely has less to do with the Amish being more pious or devout than others and more to do with the lack of opportunity. Without easy access to phones, cars, computers - the "tools of the trade" - and occupations and lives that are very structured, affairs are probably much more rare inside the Amish settlements than among the English. But, of course, the Amish are human, so they probably happen more than we might think. It was proven at trial that Eli Weaver had been visiting adult websites on his phone and corresponding with several women. This case illustrates the complexities the Amish face when deciding whether to allow new technologies.

3. Another oddity in the Raber-Weaver case was the local newspaper's - **The Wooster Daily Record** - seemingly steadfast refusal to ever utter the word "Amish" in conjunction with this case. So many media cram the "Amish angle" into stories in which the Amish presence is silly and irrelevant. But in THIS case the fact that the victim was Amish was VERY newsworthy because such occurrences are so rare. It was never clear why the local paper was so eager to tiptoe around the issue.

4. Technological trouble: So many people think the Amish have some deep aversion to technology. They don't. It's not that simple. The problems they have are less with technology and more with the "baggage" it can bring with it. A toaster or a blender, for instance, aren't viewed as inherently wrong by the Amish, it's the electricity that powers those devices that can be used to bring in TV, radio, internet, and the "whole package" of distractions brought with it that are the "problem" in their view. So they are constantly adapting, embracing, compromising, and curtailing to achieve "balance." Cell phones are a very complicated, very intensely debated issue within the church. On one hand, they present the opportunity to communicate "with control." You can turn off a cell phone, put away a cell phone, and exercise much more control - in theory - over it than a "wall mounted phone" of old. But the cell phone also can bring with it the internet and all of its problems and that seems to be the contentious issue. So out of all the ways in which Eli Weaver violated the rules of his faith: **1)** Having an affair...**2)** Murdering his wife.... **3)** Leaving his children motherless... **4)** the secrecy and lies surrounding the six year affair.all Wayne County Assistant Prosecutor Edna Boyle could say was:

"Eli Weaver was obviously not faithful to his faith and the Amish community. He did have a cell phone"

Such a quote underscores the oversimplification that many outsiders have of Amish society....Cell phones are perfectly acceptable in some Amish settlements, it is the internet and camera components that are the subject of deep debate.

The Strange Saga of Danl and Ruanna Yoder

In the summer of 2007, newspapers in Maine began reporting about a mysterious "Amish couple" that had shown up outside of Corinna, Maine, near Bangor. The couple claimed to have traveled from Tennessee by horse-drawn buggy to start a new settlement in Maine. The reporter with the local paper pretty much bought the couple's story, as she wasn't too familiar with Amish ways. But it immediately raised flags in the Amish Cook's editor's mind.

First of all, an Amish couple traveling from Tenneessee by buggy surely would generated some news coverage along the way. But there was none. And typically several Amish families move to a new area and settle. Rarely does one family up and move and just expect others to follow. Something didn't ring right.

Others began raising doubts as well.

In an exclusive interview with Oasis Newsfeatures, Corinna Town Clerk Michelle Domoulin said that initially townsfolk were touched by the Yoder's tale. "This is a wonderful community and at first our hearts really reacted, but now (the Yoders) are starting to stem curiosity in this town," Domoulin said. Corinna is a quiet hamlet west of Bangor, sandwiched between busy I-95 to the south and the less traveled Appalachian Trail winding to the north. There is a small "plain presence" in Corinna. Titus Martin is the minister of Plain Christian Fellowship, the hub of the area's settlement. "We are a small church of former Amish-Mennonites. Most Amish groups would be without electric and cars, we have electric and cars," Martin said, saying that church members don't have computers and televisions. They do dress plainly. Martin said the church began in the early 1990s by people from Ohio, Pennsylvania, and other states. The church is quite small with just a few dozen families. "In terms of church doctrine, we are very close to the Amish and Mennonites," Martin said. There is a small Amish-Mennonite school in town and even a regular scribe to *The Budget*. Another. Corinna resident, speaking anonymously, said that the Yoders story is fabricated and that they aren't welcome. Titus also distanced himself from Danl and Ruanna Yoder. Titus said that the Danl Yoder made it clear they didn't want to be a part of the Plain Christian Fellowship, but wanted to start a new church. "He wanted me to listen to him, not the other way around," Martin said, adding that he is not sure what is going to happen to them.

UPDATE - 2010:
Danl and Ruanna were spotted in Missouri. According to one eyewitness

Currently, there is an Amish Couple traveling through Missouri on bicycles, with four Scottish Terriers, who are leaving people behind with uestions. Danl and Ruanna Yoder have also apparently gone by the last names of Sinclair and Zook.

Interesting to talk with, this couple can share scriptures, beliefs, practices and values, but everyone should know that they have ulterior motive to their quest. Danl is seeking someone to finance "his new church and community" as they travel across America. People are be-friending them, supporting them, feeding them, and at times, housing them, and even learning from them as they travel. However, as this man preaches the scriptures and the importance of living by them, he is a hypocrite among hypocrites. He teaches on the sins of tattoos and how one will go to "hell" for it, yet has one on his very own ankle. Many of his teachings are just that, spoken, but not lived. Him and his wife RuAnna practice, no eating pork, head wraps, dress code, yet, they judge and condemn others and find themselves RIGHTEOUS above all.

I fear for this couple for they seem to be sacrificing so much in their lives for what they "think" is right, all the while, excluding the commandments of love and forgiveness. They appear not to have either of these two qualities in their being.

My other fear is, this couple knows the scriptures so well that they are helping to "turn" people to God with some of their teachings, and then when they become almost "tyrannical" in their teachings and beliefs, on how this affects others faith about all they have come to know through them. The couples history has been one of the same for years now

Chapter 4

AMISH CULTURAL KITCHEN SINK

What Time Is It?

In Middlefield, Ohio — A simple question – "What time is it?" — gets a bit complicated to answer sometimes.

Daylight-saving time literally puts Geauga County's Amish community on two different clocks. The Amish who spring ahead an hour, as most of the USA does, are said to be on "fast time." Those who don't live on what's called "slow time."

It's also a very confusing time that complicates everyday goings-on, such as arriving to work at the start of a shift, scheduling appointments and meeting up with friends and family.

About 10 of Geauga's 90 Amish church districts (there are about 25 - 30 families per church district) choose not to change, creating spot time zones street to street and house to house. Amish church districts are decided not just on geography but ideology. The "slow time" Amish will remain an hour behind the region's recognized time from March until October, when daylight-saving time officially ends.

Tradition guides the decision, which is made by church bishops. Some conservative Amish sects view the time-change as undue government interference on their day to day lives.

"We've always lived on this time, and there's no reason to change," says a bishop at one of the 10 slow-time districts outside of Middlefield, the hub of Geauga's Amish settlement.

The man, following tenets of Amish culture, asked that his name not be used.

This cluster of churches — as well as about 25 others in the Amish settlements spread across Holmes and Wayne counties — represent some of the few holdouts in the nation.

Opposition remains to the 60-minute move, though resistance seems to be waning. Indiana, after years of contentious debate, finally mandated daylight-saving time across the state.

Which brings us back to the Amish.

Within Geauga's slow-time church districts, numerous Amish families who work or have business dealings with the outside world have moved their clocks forward. One dairy farmer said he adjusted two years ago to synchronize with milk truck schedules.

"There's good and bad with it," the farmer says of the switch. "But it does make life easier in some ways. There's a lot less figuring."

Except for church, of course. That starts at 9 a.m. slow time on Sunday . . . or 10 a.m. on the farmer's watch.

AMISH HOLIDAYS

All Amish churches recognize the Sabbath, shuttering businesses on Sundays and spending the day with family. Beyond, Sundays, though you see wide variations in how - and what - the Amish celebrate. For the most part, Thanksgiving is considered a secular celebration and is not marked by most Amish. Pop culture influences some Amish so having a turkey on the menu on Thanksgiving is not unheard of in Amish homes, but the day is rarely observed with anything else.

JANUARY 7 - "OLD CHRISTMAS"

Today's modern Gregorian calendar establishes Christmas on Dec. 25. However, the old Julian calendar (named after the Roman Emperor) actually had Christmas later, in January. Some Amish - resistant to change - still observe Christmas on this day, which falls 12 days after December 25.

For the Amish who do still observe the occasion, the day is spent fasting with family and enjoying togetherness.

Interestingly, Ascension Day is not observed in all settlements. Amish communities near Berne and Grabill, Indiana, for instance do not mark Ascension Day. This has to do with different traditions that have evolved among the smaller Swiss settlements near Berne and the more traditional "main-line" Amish churches with solid Germanic roots elsewhere.

SPRING - ASCENSION DAY

Ascension Day is not much observed in modern times, however, it used to be a major religious day. For some Amish, Ascension Day is still observed as a holy day. On the Christian calendar this is Ascension Day, an occasion observed 40 days after each Easter, the day that Jesus Christ ascended into Heaven after the resurrection. Today, Ascension Day is primarily observed by Catholics and those in the Anglican faith. So it is curious that the Amish - who hail from a German Protestant stock - observe it. Not all Amish formally mark the day. For instance, the large Amish community near Grabill and Berne, Indiana do not observe the occasion. On the other hand, northern Indiana's mega-Amish settlement in Lagrange County, which spills into southern Michigan, does observe the holiday. In fact, many English-owned factories in the area which have a high number of Amish employees are forced to shut down on Ascension Day because so many of their workers are staying home. This just illustrates how different Amish settlements develop traditions and customs all their own. Among the Amish who do observe Ascension Day the day is a day of fasting, rest, and visiting. Children stay home from school. Families may enjoy a picnic, visit relatives, or just spend time together.

SPRING - PENTECOST MONDAY

This is an even lesser observed holiday among the Amish, occurring after every Easter. It seems to be observed most often by the Amish in Pennsylvania, however, as Amish from there have moved to other states, the day's observance seems to be spreading. It's a good Spring holiday to spend visiting with family or working in the garden.

Historical Nugget:

During the 1930s and into World War II German Fuhrer Adolf Hitler's plan was to unite German speaking peoples across the globe. The German-speaking, insular Amish didn't escape the Fuhrer's notice. There is some evidence that German agents infiltrated the Amish community in the United States to try to enlist their help in sabotage operations. The German agents quickly grew disillusioned to find that the Amish were patriotic Americans and pacifists.

TORNADOS AND THE AMISH

Since tornados tend to plow into rural areas of the Midwest most (this is due more to statistical odds than any meteorological aversion to cities), Amish communities often find themselves in the crosshairs of these fearsome storms. Often lacking radios and warning sirens, Amish often rely on subtle atmospheric clues offering hints of impending severe weather: especially still air before a storm and readings of home weather instruments.

One spring, I was visiting Lovina and Joe for the night when, after an evening of storms, we all heard the haunting wail of the nearest town's tornado sirens. The air was still outside, with barely a breeze blowing. Joe and I stepped out on the front porch. Nothing. Stillness. Out of an abundance of caution, though, we herded Lovina and all the children to the basement. Lovina keeps several mattresses down there for the children to sleep on in case a night turns stormy. Meanwhile, I called the local police non-emergency line to see what I could learn. Without access to radio, TV, or the internet, the Amish are often at the mercy of mother nature and that is just fine with them. There's an attitude that "whatever happens, happens." You can't thwart God's will. I agree with that, but sometimes if you can see it coming you can prepare. Not getting through to the police, I called my father in Ohio and had him go onto the internet to check the Michigan weather radar. He told me that the worst of the storms were passing to our south and that we were in the clear.

The LaGrange-Nappanee area of northern Indiana got raked with tornadoes in 2007, but the Amish quickly banded together to rebuild. Berne, Indiana was sucker-punched by the infamous "Palm Sunday Tornadoes" of 1965. And there have been other Amish communities clobbered, including Daviess County, Indiana.

GOVERNMENT STIMULUS

Many people have wondered what the Amish did with the government stimulus checks mailed out to most US residents during the spring of 2008. The geniuses in our government somehow thought that we as a nation could spend our way out of a recession.

Most Amish - unless they are "totally off the grid" - received checks in the mail like everyone else. The Amish, as a rule, do not accept "government subsidies" like welfare, food stamps, disability, and even, in most cases, social security. Very few Amish are on the government dole in regards to the first three. Social security. That's trickier. While the Amish are discouraged from collecting, social security is not technically a "government subsidy." Social security is money a person has paid into the system, so I am aware of some Amish who do quietly collect.

The mistake people make is thinking of the Amish as one monolithic, homogeneous sect. And while there is much, much more "groupthink" found among the Amish than other religions, in the end, they aren't much different than, say, Catholics. The official stand of the Roman Catholic is that contraceptives are not permitted. Italy, on the other hand, has one of the lowest birthrates in Europe. Draw your own conclusions. My point is that the Amish are like anyone else, some will "tow the line" of the church in every way. Others will fudge here and there. You find that in any religion. So back to the issue of the rebates:

I was visiting one Amish community recently and the issue of the rebates came up and a woman said to me: "I heard about those checks, but the bishop told us that you couldn't put it in savings, you have to spend it." I laughed. And said: "No, the government WANTS you to spend it, but you are allowed to do whatever you want with the money." So there is a little misinformation in the Amish community about the checks, but, at least in this settlement, the checks had the tacit approval of the bishop. Are most Amish technically supposed to accept the checks? Probably not. Are most Amish - who are normal humans - going to see the check in their mail box and rip it up? Probably not.

FUN FACT - STEERING COMMITTEE

While there is no formal church structure in the Amish faith, in 1966 a group of Amish bishops decided to start a "steering committee" to help guide overall church direction and to facilitate discussion on issues facing the faith.

DO THE AMISH PLAY MUSICAL INSTRUMENTS?

In most Amish settlements, musical instruments are forbidden. Playing an instrument would be considered worldly and contrary to the spirit of *Glassenheit* (humility). In some communities, however, harmonicas seem to have gained at least a tacit acceptance. The reasons for this are unclear, but they are handheld and simple, which makes them a very minimalist instrument.

WHO ARE THE GERMAN BAPTISTS?

While the German Baptists are a "plain" church, their theological roots begin in a religious movement known as Pietism. The Amish, Hutterites, and Mennonites are all Anabaptists. The end result, though, of the Pietist movement is a church that at least on the surface looks a lot like the Amish.

People in Ohio and Indiana, which have large populations of Old German Baptist Church members (not Old ORDER), repeatedly and mistakenly refer to these people as "Amish." The dress is vagely similar. Women wear head-coverings, but they are an opaque white. Men usually where denim, suspenders, and have neatly trimmed beards. The GB's also have their own "one room" parochial schools. And, unlike the Amish, the GBs have a church building (meetinghouse) where they worship. The GBs also drive cars (usually dark-colored) and have electricity, although most don't have television or radio.

The Old GB church has members in western Ohio, eastern Indiana, near Quinter, Kansas, and near Modesto, California.

But then there are the OLD ORDER GERMAN BAPTIST BRETHREN. This church split from the main GB church back in 1921 over the acceptance of automobiles. These GBs remain, in a sense, "frozen in time" in 1921. They do have electricity, but no TV or radio and they don't drive cars. These GBs still use the horse and buggy. The Old Order German Baptist churches are few in number. There are three church districts near Bradford, Ohio. Each church district has about 40 families. There are a handful of other Old Order Gbs elsewhere, the largest group is near Delphi, Indiana. The group near Delphi split from the Bradford, Ohio GBs over some other theological differences back in the 1930s.

WHO ARE THE HUTTERITES?

The Hutterites are a lesser-known, smaller-in-number Anabaptist group, closely connected to the Amish and Mennonites. The Hutterites originated in the same Anabaptist movement that gave rise to the Amish and Mennonite faiths. The single biggest difference between the Hutterites and other Anabaptists is their communal existence. The Amish are very individualistic and the acquiring of wealth is encouraged. The Hutterites resemble the Amish in dress, culinary culture, rejection of technology, and gender role assignments, but the wealth and resources of the group are completely shared.

The Hutterites are found primarily in the Dakotas, southern Canada, and Montana. Interestingly, there is one large Amish community in Montana also (opposite end of the state from the Hutterites and there is little interaction between the groups despite their commonalities). The Hutterites have been able to stop the shift away from agrarianism longer than the Amish have been. Hutterites have successful hog-raising operations and turkey farms.

Like the Amish, the Hutterites generally do not want to be photographed and in 2009 fought the Alberta provincial government in court over a requirement that Hutterites have photos on their drivers license. Unlike the Amish, Hutterites do drive cars. The Hutterites lost that fight in court.

WHO ARE THE SHAKERS?

Some people make the mistake of lumping the Shakers, Quakers, Mennonites, Dunkers, Amish, Amana Colonies, Hutterites, and other Utopian offshoots into one group. In fact, there are deep differences between most of the ones I just mentioned. It is true that there is a general "philosophical umbrella" that most of them share, but that is about it. Shakers and Hutterites for instance are far more communal than the individualistic Amish. And the differences don't end there.

Embracing technology

Despite their use of horse-powered transportation, their ban on television and their preference for a style of wide-brimmed hat that dates to the 16th century, the Amish do not prohibit the use of modern technology per se.

What's important to them is how those innovations might affect the health and cohesion of their own family and community, said sociologist Donald B. Kraybill, author of several books on the Amish.

"They do not have a negative opinion of technology. In other words, they are not Luddites that say technology is bad," said Kraybill, on the faculty of Elizabethtown and Messiah colleges. "They selectively use [it]."

WANT MORE INFORMATION?

Mennonite Historical Society, which maintains an extensive genealogical library. Their address is 2215 Millstream Road, Lancaster, PA 17602. Telephone: (717)393-9745.

Driving with the Amish

Reprinted with permission from The Ohio State University

Driving in Amish communities is different than driving on other rural or urban highways. In Amish communities you will see horse-drawn buggies or equipment on the roadway as they travel to town or the fields. Statistics show that more than 65 percent of all traffic deaths occur in rural areas and 50 percent of those deaths are on country roads. Ohio reports, on average, more than 120 buggy accidents a year.

Rural Roads are Not City Streets

Rural roads are often narrower or may vary in width more than city streets. A narrow road give you less room to maneuver and can be especially dangerous when passing horse-drawn vehicles. A loose gravel or grass berm area can also be hazardous. Open ditches along rural roads are often deep and close to the road. Seemingly open roadways may have sharp dips or unexpected turns. In cold weather, a road shaded by trees or buildings may be icy because then sun has not shone on that part of the roadway. Blind corners created by wooded areas, corn fields or other tall crops are also hazardous.

Normal speeds for horse-drawn buggies range between five and eight miles per hour. Horse-drawn vehicles may be even slower when pulling large farm equipment or when crossing intersections because horses are not tractors or cars and will eventually become tired. Another hazard to consider is restricted vision from the driver of the horse-drawn vehicle. When pulling large loads of hay or other equipment, drivers may not be able to see cars behind them. Car drivers, therefore, need to be extra cautious when passing horse-drawn farm equipment. To avoid other possible collisions, car drivers should anticipate left hand turns made by horse-drawn vehicles into fields and driveways.

Even the Fastest Horse is Slow Compared to Your Car

Knowing "closure time" is a safety factor that could save lives. "Closure time" is the time a driver has to recognize and respond when coming upon other vehicles. Leave some space between your vehicle and a buggy stopped at a stop sign or light. Buggies may back up a few feet after coming to a complete stop. A good rule of thumb is to stop your vehicle far enough back so that you can see where the rear wheels of the buggy touch the road. This should give you 10-12 feet of clearance between you and the buggy. This rule does not apply to drivers of vans or mini-vans; they will have to remember to always STAY BACK.

Imagine traveling at 55 mph and coming upon a car traveling at 45 mph that is 500 feet (about 1/10 of mile) ahead. After six seconds, you will have 412 feet to react before colliding with that car. However, if traveling at 55 mph and coming upon a horse-drawn vehicle traveling a 5 mph that is 500 feet ahead, you will have only 44 feet to react before colliding in the same six seconds. The car would hit the horse-drawn vehicle in just 6 seconds. Therefore, immediately upon seeing the slow moving vehicle emblem, slow down and prepare to pass with caution.

This is a slow-moving vehicle sign and should be mounted on all farm machinery, including road construction equipment and animal-drawn vehicles. The sign should signal motor vehicle drivers to slow down. Vehicles displaying the slow-moving vehicle sign are prohibited by law to go faster than 25 mph.

When approaching and passing a horse-drawn vehicle, remember that horses are unpredictable and even the most road-safe horse can spook at a fast-moving motor vehicle. Be sure to slow down and give buggies and horse-drawn equipment plenty of room when passing. Only pass when legal and safe.

The information on this page was developed by Dr. T.L. Bean, Ms. A.J. Yarosh, Mr. T.J. Lawrence, and R.E. James. Reviewed by Dr. J.A. Gliem, Mr. R.L. Clason and R. Elaine Hitchcock. Issued in futherance of Cooperative Extension work, Acts of May 8 and June 30, 1914, in cooperation with the U.S. Department of Agriculture, Keith L. Smith, Director, Ohio State University Extension, The Ohio State University.

AMISH BUGGY SAFETY GUIDE:

Slow-moving vehicles and high-speed cars pose an increasing danger on the congested rural roads of Amish country.

According to the Ohio Department of transportation, there were 140 car-buggy accidents in 1998 causing 4 deaths. Between 1990 and 1997 more than 500 vehicle-buggy crashes were reported, 66% were caused by a motorist following too closely. According to the Lancaster Country Planning Commission, there were 68 vehicle-buggy accidents in Pennsylvania in 1996 (38 in Lancaster Country). Leacock Township lead the list for accidents.

The Ohio Department of Transportation has been holding public meetings in 1999 to educate the Amish on better buggy lighting, etc. One of the suggestions from the Ohio meetings has been the use of reflective ankle bracelets for horses. In November 1999, Kentucky Amish were also holding safety meetings regarding having proper reflectors and lights on their buggies. Many other states also held meetings. Between 300-400 Amish have attended but because of the rural locations of the Amish communities it is nearly impossible to reach everyone.

While most states and counties are trying to ensure safer travel for both types of vehicles, an area near Hillsdale/Camden is working against safety. The country road commissioners will not post signs warning of slow moving vehicles, even though the Amish offered to pay for them. The commissioners say they will post the signs if the Amish will use reflectors. There have been numerous accidents in the area with damage to Amish and English alike during 1999. Michigan law required buggies to have battery-operated lights, a white reflective strip, and a round reflective red light the size of an orange.

There are still problems in some states and Amish communities:

- Eight men were fined $328 for refusal to attach the slow moving vehicle signs to their buggies. These men belong to the Old Order Amish community in Iowa.
- Because their religion forbids the use of bright colors, the conservative Swartzentruber group has refused to put the slow moving vehicle sign on their buggies. However, they have

compromised by putting brighter lanterns and reflective tape on their buggies.

Driving used to be done from the right side of the buggy to avoid the danger of driving into a ditch. But today driving is mostly done from the left side.

The use of certain equipment on buggies is required by law in most states and providence's. Check your state regulations for their requirements. Equipment used on the buggies will vary depending on what is permitted by their Amish community. When this equipment is used properly, it allows motor vehicle drivers to easily identify the buggy from a great distance. Buggies should be readily identifiable both by night and day and should be well-lighted.

The vehicle drivers must also follow the rules of the road by not passing in no passing zones, follow posted speed limits, and use caution at crest of hills and bends.

The following items are recommended and in some states required by law.

- Mirrors - one placed on the drivers side (left side of buggy). If the driver sits on the right, a mirror should also be placed on the right side.
- Windows - windows should be placed in line of vision if buggies are closed
- Reflectors - several round red reflectors should be placed on back of the buggy
- Reflective tape - tape should outline the sides of buggy
- Slow-moving vehicle emblem - should be placed on the rear of buggy
- Harness - worn equipment should be replaced
- Lights - 2 lights on both the front and back are recommended. Various communities use different types of lighting such as buggy lanterns, portable dry cell battery lights, or wet cell wired battery lights (this type is becoming the most popular in most communities)

All equipment should be periodically checked and replaced when needed. Emblems fade. Worn harnesses break causing lost of control of the horse. Mirrors should be large enough so that the whole road is visible. Battery lights should be kept charged. If lanterns are used, be sure globes are clean.

Reducing the speed limit in these areas would be an easy and inexpensive start to the problem. Ohio has added or widen berms on the roadways is some areas but this is a costly project.

AMISH NEWSPAPERS

Forget fancy graphics, color photos, and hard news. My favorite newspaper in the whole world is probably "**The Budget.**" This is a national newspaper distributed in Amish communities and mailed to Amish homes that subscribe to it. The paper's format is simple: Amish writers (known as scribes) volunteer to report the "news" from their community. With a general absence of phones and email among the Anabaptists, the Budget - based in Sugarcreek, Ohio - still serves as a vital source of news and information. You can either subscribe to the Budget or sometimes buy it in stores. A tiny grocery store in Adams County, Ohio used to sell it and I'd sometimes drive a couple of hours from my house just to snag a copy. Yoder's Restaurant in Bradenton, Florida sells it as do numerous other businesses in and around Amish country. The writing is very endearing and honest, which makes it a very refreshing read.

Often the writers will use the space to discuss newsworthy items of importance to them. For instance, several years ago Indiana started cracking down on "unlicensed taxis."

One Amish writer wrote in the Budget in 2008:

"We are having quite a problem with the cops stopping all our taxi drivers because of not having an I-DOT (Indiana Dept. of Transportation) number on their vans. Some are not even allowed to take their loads on home. The big guys at Wal-Mart and Aldis are getting very upset as they are losing lots of customers because of it. Also heard the Wal-Mart guys are

thinking of suing the state cops for taking up parking spots when they are not paying customers. It is causing quite a ruckus among some of the Amish around here but it doesn't affect us as we hardly ever get a driver."

Another writes:

The state troopers are really cracking down on the van drivers with this law that went in effect concerning their DOT insurance and the whole ball of wax that drivers are supposed to have. Someone asked a trooper what we Amish should do if we can't have drivers to take us anywhere. His answer was: "change your lifestyle," which sounds rather radical.

Hopefully some sort of compromise can be reached, but as of this book's publication nothing seemed close. I do think some regulation is probably in order, but snide comments from troopers (if that story is true) doesn't really help matters any.

Another Amish newspaper that might not be as familiar to readers of this book is "*Die Botschaft*." Published in Pennsylvania, this paper serves the more conservative Amish communities that find the Budget a bit too mainstream. *Die Botschaft* is German for "The Message." Die Botschaft has English and Pennsylvania Dutch language versions and shares a similar format to its more well-known cousin, The Budget. News of farm accidents, weddings, and bountiful garden harvests permeate the pages.

The newspaper, which preaches the pacifism that the Amish espouse, had a difficult time with the tragic school shooting in Nickel Mines, Pennsylvania in 2006. At first the editor struggled with whether to even mention it. Eventually a decision was made to print a simple "Thank You" on the front page for all the outreach from the non-Amish community. Then it was back to the regular rhythm of life in the Amish. That, in the end, could have been the best tribute to the shooting victims.

PROVERBS

The Amish use proverbs in everyday speech, especially when talking or teaching children. The sayings promote hard work, character development, respect for others, and personal sanctity.

Amish culture (ideas, customs, skills, etc.) that has been learned through the years from their ancestor's lifestyle of simplicity, has passed virtually unchanged through the generations and provides an ideal base for the continual use of proverbs. These proverbs are time-tested lessons from past Amish generations of how to lead a morally sound lifestyle. Using the phrases frequently prevents the Amish from forgetting the sayings, and most importantly, the lessons they hold.

The following are proverbs that are put to use from raising children to helping with faith:

- "Take all you want, eat all you take."
- "You can preach a better sermon with your life than with your lip."
- "A man who gives his children habits of industry provides for them better than by giving them a fortune."
- "Children need models more than they need critics."
- "The apple will not roll far away from its tree."
- "Such as the tree is, such is the fruit."
- "Bend the tree while it is young; when it is old it is too late."
- "No dream comes true until you wake up and go to work."
- "He that rises late must trot all day, and shall scarce overtake his business at night."
- "It is better to suffer wrong than to do it. And happier to be sometimes cheated than to never trust."
- "A handful of patience is worth more than a bushel of brains."
- "Adopt the pace of nature; her secret is patience."
- "You can't make cider without apples."

- "Don't count your eggs before they are laid."
- "No one is useless in this world who lightens the burden of it for someone else."
- "How pleasant and good it is when brothers are peaceable, when their doings are in agreement."
- "Give every man your ear, but few your voice take each man's censure, but reserve your judgment."
- "If you want good advice, consult an old man."
- "Sometimes God calms the storm, but sometimes God lets the storm rage and calms his child."
- "The gem cannot be polished without friction, nor the man perfected without trials."
- "Courage is fear that has said its prayers."
- "One lie brings the next one with it."
- "Getting sick is easy; getting well is the trick."

FUNERALS

Funerals are obviously grief-filled events for the Amish, just like anyone. But the Amish also view a funeral as the final step of this journey and the first step of a much better one. The Amish are grounded by a deep faith that the afterlife is a more joyous place, which tends to temper the grief normally found at funerals. Answers to a few frequent reader questions about funerals:

1. The Amish do embalm their dead. That's a question I get asked often. I think local laws and ordinances trump any other beliefs the Amish might have about whether to embalm or not.
2. There is a viewing held at the home of the deceased. The viewing can often last up to 48 hours as it takes a long time for word to spread in the Amish community about a death and time to make preparations for travel, find a driver, etc. Family members will stay with the body even throughout the night as visitors come through.

3. A funeral is held at the home with burial at a typical Amish cemetery. Some Amish churches are trending towards holding funerals in "community buildings," self-contained structures used for other functions. This is causing some controversy as some fear this is the first step in moving away from home worship and into formal church buildings, like the Mennonites and other more liberal Anabaptist groups.

BIRTHDAYS

Birthdays are also celebratory occasions among the Amish. Presents are exchanged and usually a cake is served, along with some ice cream. Like most events, the Amish are low-key about birthdays. You usually won't see surprise parties (where would the guests park the buggies so that no one sees them!?) and a bunch of gifts. The event is usually just a "cake break" from the busy week.

This is a delicious, moist chocolate cake recipe that Lovina uses for some of her children's birthdays. It's a great alternative to a box cake or store-bought.

> 2 eggs
> 2 cups brown sugar
> 1 /2 cup oil
> 1 /2 cup milk
> 2 cups flour
> 1 teaspoon baking soda
> 1/2 teaspoon baking powder
> 4 teaspoons cocoa
> 3 /4 cup boiling water

Mix well and bake 30 to 35 minutes at 350. Let cool and then add frosting.

DO THE AMISH VOTE?

The old adage is that you can't complain if you don't vote. And that is why the Amish don't complain much: they rarely vote.

The Amish simply don't get involved in the machinations of government and they view voting as another extension of that. Still, there are rare occasions when the Amish *will* show up at the polls. The issue that really fires the Amish up is an issue that would send most of us into snores: zoning. If the possibility of peaceful, pastoral rural land being zoned into "big box store" land exists, and the issue is on the ballot, then the Amish will often register to vote. The Amish have shocked a few developers through the years by unexpectedly turning out at the polls and swinging an election. So the rare issues that would fire up the Amish to go vote are often very, very, very local issues. The Amish will also weigh in sometimes on local levies such as for the volunteer fire department or a mental health campaign. The Amish don't typically participate in Presidential or Congressional contests.

Meanwhile, with Ohio and Pennsylvania both being hotly contested Presidential battleground states in 2000 and 2004, Republicans saw an opportunity among the Amish for votes. Amish sympathy lies heavily with the pro-life movement which most often aligns itself with the Republican party. Realizing this, GOP operatives scoured Ohio's Amish country in 2004 trying to register Amish voters. President Bush even took the unprecedented step of meeting with some Amish while on the campaign trail in 2004. While Amish sympathies do lie with the pro-life, anti-abortion movement they are also pacifists and were disturbed by the war in Iraq. Of course Democrats largely held the cards of the anti-war vote. So the attempt at getting Amish to vote in the Presidential race in 2004 was largely a wash. Had the war not been going on, the GOP could have theoretically made significant inroads into the Amish. By the 2008 Obama-McCain content, both parties pretty much ignored the potential Amish vote.

WHAT IS RUMSPRINGA?

Teenagers. Simply utter the word and images of moody, rowdy, unpredictable, fashion-challenged youth appear in most minds. Teenagers around the world share similar desires, feelings, and needs to test boundaries. Amish children are no different. Some pass through their teen years relatively uneventfully and other Amish adolescents really push the boundaries. A term often used to describe this rebellious period is "rumspringa." This is a German word which can be roughly translated as "running around." Rumspringa, for some Amish youth, is a period of running around, testing limits, exploring. In short, it is the same as any other teen. Among the Amish, however, the need to test boundaries may be more pressing, because once one becomes a young adult (age 18 - 21, depending on the community), they will have to make a decision whether to formally join the church through baptism. Once a member, they must adhere to a strict moral code and set of religious rules. So the teenage years are a time to experiment and explore before choosing whether to commit to such a lifestyle.

Media and pop culture have made rumspringa into more of an event than it is in reality. Documentaries such as "Devil's Playground," while insightful, may give the impression that all Amish adolescents are raiding the liquor cabinet and seeking smokes. Not true. Do some? Absolutely.

Rumspringa, despite the forays into alcohol and wild parties, serves an important sociological purpose, which is to let the insulated Amish youth experience the wider world without fear of parental penalty. More often than not, after sticking their big toe in the waters of the world, the Amish youth decide to stay in the religion of their upbringing.

RECOMMENDED READING:

"Rumspringa: To Be or Not to Be Amish," by Tom Shactman. The book can be purchased from your local bookseller.

UNIQUE EVENT

There are many opportunities to interact with the Amish, but these are usually in more formal settings like a bakery or an auction. The Adams County Ohio Amish Bird Symposium is one of the few events where English and Amish unite for the pure enjoyment of a topic, in this case: birding in Ohio. The event, held each March as migratory bird season ramps up, is sponsored by the Cincinnati Museum Center's Edge of Appalachia Preserve and the local Amish community.

Roman Mast, the Amish originator of the event, usually opens the event with warm, witty remarks about his love of birding. One year's symposium featured Dennis Kline, an Amish birding enthusiast, who delivered an engaging talk. Kline's presentation was a folksy mix of bird experiences and insight into Amish life.

"There are those who look at the children in the back of our buggy and ask if they are deprived, without television or the internet. Well you can't feel deprived of something if you've never had it," Kline said, explaining the richness of Amish life without modern technological toys.

The Amish presentations are usually followed by some very informative and entertaining non-Amish speakers. One year author and NPR commentator Julie Zickefoose spoke.

Activities take place under the rules of the Amish, which means over 250 of us in a big barn without electricity or running water. But none of those amenities were missed. A highlight of the day was a lunch prepared by some skilled Amish cooks (feeding 250 people, no big deal....Sunday church services often require double the food). The event also features a family flair with my sister-in-law, Susan Williams, education director of Raptor Inc. in Cincinnati, bringing some her feathered friends to the symposium. All of these events were held against the ruggedly beautiful backdrop of the Adams County hill country. Winding ribbons of road disappear into the folds of these mini-mountains, with names like Tater Ridge and Tranquilty. Adams County is definitely worth a visit and I'm already looking forward to next year's bird symposium!

WHAT IS A DEPRESSION GARDEN?

In November of 1996, The Amish Cook wrote about "Depression Gardens." I had never heard of a "Depression Garden", but it seemed that many of our readers had. Many readers had childhood memories of making this colorful craft at home, I think it was something to entertain and enjoy during the most wanting days of the Great Depression, hence its name.

DEPRESSION GARDE

six small stones or lumps of coal (no larger than an egg)
Place stones in the bottom of a shallow glass bowl and mix together in the following in a separate bowl:
6 liquid tablespoons of liquid bluing (not powder)
6 tablespoons of salt
1 tablespoon of household ammonia

Pour ammonia mixture over stones. Do not cover. Keep solution at same level by "feeding" it with equal parts water and ammonia. Pour down the sides of the bowl, not over the stones when adding. A drop of food coloring on each stone will add color. The flowers will grow out of the bowl. This solution will damage furniture, so watch closely.

CROSSING OVER: THE STORY OF THE MOSERS

I met Bill Moser when he was 4 years old. I was 4 years old too. We lived three houses apart in a Livonia subdivision, a new one—most of the lawns were still dirt when we met. If it's possible for a place to be extreme middle class, Livonia was it back then. No visible poor people. No visible rich people. No visible ethnic people. Even today, Livonia has the highest percentage of Caucasians of any city with more than 100,000 residents in the United States.

Sometimes I wonder if the homogeneous nature of our town, the monoculture, inspired Bill's curiosity about other people, his desire to look into other worlds and understand and adopt the good that was there. Don't know, but here's something I remember. Bill was the first person I knew who was really into soul music. Not in a fake "trying to be a brother" sort of way, but just in a natural "I'm really into this sound" sort of way.

One time, when we were 16, he bought us tickets to a Marvin Gaye concert at Olympia Stadium. We each took dates. This was 1974; the Detroit race riots were just seven years behind us. The racial divide was perhaps greater than ever, and people in Livonia were afraid to go downtown. But Bill loved the music, and he intuitively understood that people getting together for a Marvin Gaye concert—"How Sweet It Is to Be Loved by You" and "Let's Get It On"—were looking to make love not problems. And his 16-year-old's instinct proved right. I remember seeing about 10 white people in the sold-out arena of 15,000, and everybody went out of their way to make us feel welcome.

Now follow along as we fast-forward. Bill goes to University of Detroit to study architecture. He graduates. Bill marries Tricia, the Catholic girl he went to the Marvin Gaye concert with. She, by now, is an occupational therapist, having graduated from Wayne State University. I am the best man in the wedding. When my wife and I get married a few years later, Bill is best man in our wedding; Tricia is a bridesmaid.

Now five years further, Bill and Tricia are living in Grosse Pointe Park. Bill has a lead role in designing a building in downtown Birmingham. Soon, he starts his own construction-design company. The couple is becoming increasingly religious, and they join an evangelical church.

My wife and I have moved to Minneapolis. We do not become increasingly religious. Due to place and lifestyle, we drift apart from the Mosers.

Skip ahead to 1999.

My family has by now moved back to Traverse City. I get a call from Tricia inviting us to visit their small farm near Ovid, east of St. Johns. It turns out I am heading to Detroit Metropolitan Airport in a few days to pick up my kids, who are returning from Minneapolis. It is height of summer, crazy busy, but their house is on the way. I pull off the highway, steer down dirt roads and pull up in the driveway. I see not a car, but instead a black buggy, as in horse and buggy. I get out of my car. I stand for a moment in the lush July dusk. A horse grazes in a small paddock. Chest-high grasses with seed-tops tinged in purple twilight fill a low swale. The orangey glow of propane lamps illuminates the house windows. I hear quiet. I feel peace.

I knock on the door, and Bill answers with Trish and his six children crowded round. Bill has a beard, suspenders, plain blue pants and shirt. Tricia wears a cap, an ankle-length dress. We hug. A self-conscious smile crosses Bill's face. "Well," he says, "do you think we've gone crazy?"

And one last time travel. Forward to 2009. Bill and Tricia have by now moved farther North, to an Amish community near Cadillac. More broadly, America has entered a troubled time. The Dow has fallen from 14,100 to 7,500, millions of people are losing their homes, debt-fueled consumerism has veered into a very mucky ditch, and some say Americans are taking a new look at what's really important, about our culture possibly making a long-term change to a simpler lifestyle. I head to Cadillac to talk to the people who have the simplest life I know and ask them to tell me why they rejected today's American way and crossed over to Amish.

We meet at the end of January, a 12-degree morning when snow covers the ground and a brilliant blue sky opens above. When I pull up, I see 20-foot-high towers of shipping pallets rising from a paved lot near an outbuilding. I'm pondering how they stack the pallets so high without motored equipment when the garage door opens, and one of the couple's sons drives out on a forklift.

Bill gives me a brief shop tour before we head into the house to talk. The home business that the Mosers do now is building pallets, which they sell to an Amish pallet distributor in McBain. The Amish limit their use of electricity, but not all are opposed to mechanical automation. I watch as Aaron, 18, and Timothy, 20, load the pneumatic pallet-making machine (the air pressure powered by a diesel engine) with wood and then push a button. Bam, bam, bam, bam, out comes a pallet on the other end. Eventually each son will decide on a home business of his own. Aaron is experimenting by selling battery-operated headlamps locally and through mail order.

We head into the house, an old farmhouse that the family renovated and expanded to about 3,000 square feet. Tricia has coffee ready in a stovetop percolator. The cream on the table came from their Jersey cow. Sarah, 14, is home because she graduated from Amish school last year; today she's sewing something for a wedding gift.

The two youngest boys are in school, a short walk down the road. Sunlight washes in through a south window that faces the road, and periodically, horse-drawn carriages and sleighs drive by.

People with even the most basic knowledge of Amish life understand that living Amish involves every aspect of life—religion, family, culture and work—and the Mosers' tale touches upon each of these things. But religion is foremost, and this is where the couple's evolution began.

"We were in the routine for 13 years," Bill says, looking back on their days in Grosse Pointe. "We went to a Protestant church, we worked with the youth group, our children went there," he says. But after a change in pastors, the church changed. The new pastors seemed overly interested in growing the membership and in defining the way parishioners related to Jesus.

"More and more I questioned, why don't we just do what Jesus says?" Bill says. In other words, take the Bible at face value, a plain interpretation that would guide daily life.

Then on a Sunday near Christmas during the Gulf War of the early 1990's, something happened that elevated their concerns. During the regular church service, military color guard carrying rifles marched in formation up the center aisle of the church. They took position between the altar and the pews, and they led the parishioners in patriotic songs.

"It was very troubling," Tricia says. "We talked about it in the car on the way home." Tricia proclaims a love for her country, but her religious beliefs guide her here. "What really bothered me is that my Christian nephew could be called up to go to another country and kill another Christian, or worse, kill a non-Christian who won't go to heaven."

About this same time, the couple began wanting to move to the countryside—maybe find a small school for their kids, or maybe home school—so they bought land in Michigan's Thumb. Bill designed the house and bought lumber from an Amish man who ran a sawmill in Gladwin, near a cottage the Moser family has owned since the 1950's.

Bill had noticed the Amish moving to the Gladwin countryside in the late 1970's. "I saw fallow land being farmed again, decrepit farmhouses being fixed up," he says. "And I noticed that the people made do with what they had."

One time Bill was canoeing down a narrow river near Gladwin, and a massive Belgian draft horse crashed out of the shoreline thicket. It splashed across the river directly in front of him, and then disappeared on the other side. The horse was an Amish workhorse, and looking back on the moment—the tight quarters of the river, the water, the tremendous, muscular presence of the horse careening by, then vanishing—it's tempting to think of the event as a foreshadowing of the force that the Amish would play in his life.

The Amish sawmill owner, Joni Mast, was a lifelong Amish, friendly and curious about the Mosers and their Christian beliefs. "He gave me a statement of their faith. It looked like what I believed in, nothing there that would look strange to most Christians," Bill says. He especially liked the Amish idea that daily acts—the moment by moment things we do—not words, are the true expression of faith.

"If I shake somebody's hand and say, 'God be with you,' and then walk away, what have I really done?" he says. For Bill the statement of faith put to rest concerns that the Amish community is a cult.

And there was something else about Joni Mast's life that made a big impression on the Mosers. They saw that the man's children were with the parents throughout the day. The family did not have the 10- or 12-hour daily separation between children and parents that many American families accept as a part of 21st-century existence—babies dropped off at daycare at 6:30 a.m. and picked up at 6:30 p.m.

"I'd been thinking for a long time that I wanted to shrink my world, create a life where work, recreation, family and religion were all one, a whole, not so fragmented," he says. Bill went home and looked up Amish in the encyclopedia. He learned that the Amish were part of the Anabaptist Reformation and had been around since the 1600's.

Bill and Tricia's curiosity kept drawing them closer to the Amish as the months went by. The couple hired Amish builders to frame their home in the Thumb. Eventually they visited the farm of a family that had recently left mainstream life and joined an Amish community in Manton, just north of Cadillac. The visit remains one of the most memorable points in Bill and Tricia's journey.

It was a fall day, and the Moser family—by now five children, the oldest 12, the youngest an infant—pulled up to Alfred Gingerich's home about the time of evening chores. Gingerich and his 10 children were in the barn milking cows by hand. The barn was a traditional barn with the cows tied in their stalls in the lower level. Bill remembers the children carrying milk pails through the barn and dumping them into the bulk tank. He remembers the sound of the milk pinging into the metal pail, the smell of silage mixed with the scent of cows and straw and manure. He remembers the family singing. One of the children would start a song, and the others would join in on old English hymns.

"These people were together as a family, enjoying each others' company," Bill says. "This was the vision I had for my family, their work, their religion and life all integrated together."

The Amish call converts to their faith "Seekers," and the term seemed so remarkably apt for the Mosers. Bill and Tricia drove to Ovid to enter the Amish life in 1999. "We pulled up in the driveway with a rental truck and there were about a half dozen families there to help us unload," Bill says. He returned the truck and drove back to Ovid, and that was the last time he drove a car.

The Mosers had considered their decision a multitude of times, had prayed for direction, had a clear understanding of what they were doing, but still there have been moments when they've doubted the decision to become Amish.

The most tenuous arrived in 2004. The church they belonged to in Ovid was breaking up over issues related to the control of the church and differing views of the direction it should take. "It was quite a let down. But we learned the Amish are a people like any other people, with the same issues," Bill says.

People from Ovid went in different directions, joined different types of churches. "We wondered if we should go back to what we were doing before, or join a more progressive church, like a Mennonite church, and get an automobile again." But instead, they moved to Cadillac to join a more established Amish community there.

Recently, another time of questioning arose. Good friends who lived in a nearby Amish community, and who were also Seekers, decided to leave the Amish and joined a Mennonite church in Kentucky. What made their move troubling for the Mosers is that this family's story of leaving mainstream America and their reasons for becoming Amish was a touchstone in the Mosers' own decision, because their reasons were so similar.

The greatest challenge Seekers face tends not to be longing for artifacts from their former life, like, say, a car or a computer. The biggest challenge is Seekers may feel like ex-patriots from the United States living in an Amish nation; they don't share decades of life story and customs with the people they live among.

And above all, Seekers struggle with the language, a German dialect called Pennsylvania Dutch. Language is of course important in assimilating to any foreign culture, but for Seekers the issue goes far beyond learning how to say, "Where is the bathroom?" The Seekers' new religion is often discussed in the new language, and language becomes a barrier to what the Seekers most seek: a nuanced and in-depth understanding of the Amish faith and continued growth in their spirituality.

The Mosers' friends left the Amish for a Mennonite church that offered a sermon in English every week. The Mosers' church offers sermons in English every other week and translators for people who need them during the German services. Bill and Tricia have worked hard to learn the tongue. Originally they had hoped to speak fluently. But now, Tricia hopes only that one day she'll be able to understand what's being said.

"I don't know that we'll ever reach a point where we feel totally immersed in the culture," Bill concedes. "But our children already do. They grew up with the language and completely understand it."

When Bill and Tricia have faced their low points and discussed with their children the notion of changing churches, the kids have always said, "We want to keep doing what we have been doing." And the older kids who have the choice have said, "If you do that, you will be doing it without us," Bill says.

The heights of the couple's spiritual year, and when they feel most immersed in the community, comes during communion service, which happens twice a year, and in particular during a ritual in which each church member washes another member's feet. The bible encourages the practice, Bill says, but few Christian sects perform the ritual. Church members go up in pairs, men with men, women with women.

"You take turns, you wash and dry the person's feet and then they do yours," Tricia says. "It's an expression of love and service to one another."

Communion is also a time when the community reviews the Amish statement of faith, a 400-year-old document that lays out what's expected of community members. They also review what technology is okay and what is not. While there are general guidelines that apply to all Amish, each church writes its own agreement to deal with some particulars. Amish keep their churches small, say fewer than 30 families, so there are hundreds of such statements serving the 300,000 or so Amish in America today.

We have talked a long time, and by now it is mid-afternoon. The youngest boys come home from school. "We had a runaway today," Jacob says, referring to a horse that spooked and smashed up a buggy—which had no passengers at the time. An Amish girl knocks on the door wanting to buy a headlamp. Outside the window, I see buggies going by driven by kids who look to be about 10 years old. Behind some, boys drag on their bellies on the icy road. I'm reminded of Bill and me at 14, hanging out at stop signs in winter, waiting to grab on to the rear bumpers of cars as they took off, pulling us sliding down Ellen Drive.

Like anyone else in America, I'm curious about the Amish and technology. I think of the forklift, a power saw Timothy used in the shop, the battery-operated headlamp business. I think of the phone network that Amish use extensively to pass news—the couple learned of the Pennsylvania Amish school shooting within minutes of it happening. I ask Bill and Tricia to clarify, because the boundaries seem fluid.

A main defining goal is keeping out technology that weakens the family or the community, Bill says. Cars, for example. The decision to not own automobiles is largely a result of a desire to keep men working at the home whenever possible. But the Amish can hire people to drive them places. Bill concedes that he hires drivers often to take him to Marion or Cadillac.

"I'm at the upper end of the use scale," he says. He should be riding his bike—the nearest town, Marion, is just six miles away. But he shrugs it off—he is, after all, a son of the Motor City.

Or consider the issue of how propane should be supplied in a home—piping or small tanks. Some felt if propane were piped throughout the home, it would be too easy to have a light in every room, so family members would be more likely to read in their own bedrooms and spend less time together in the evening. I was reminded of a mainstream woman I once knew who traced the breakup of her family to when her husband brought home a television for each kid's bedroom. Piping was ultimately allowed because of fire concerns about propane tanks in the home.

Or another: a member wanted to purchase a round baler for hay, which enables a farmer to do hay solo. But some in the community felt that the team approach to hay is an important part of neighborliness and keeping community bonds strong. Eventually they allowed the baler, but only one farmer uses it.

And there are other places where I'm surprised to find technology in the conversation. Tricia says a photographer shot a story at the Montana Amish school where their eldest son teaches. "You can see it on the Internet," she says. The community has not officially discussed Internet use.

I try to think of the most out-there technological dilemma I know of. "I read that people who have had a child die are the most ardent activists pushing for the cloning of humans—what do you think of that?" I ask.

Bill looks to the ceiling. He pauses for a while. "You see, what am I even able to do with that information?" he says. "I have no way to influence that. It does not affect my life. There is a passage in the Bible that says, 'do not be overly concerned with rumors of war.' And it implies do not be overly concerned with distant issues that you cannot change. Like global warming. I can send money to some far off group in Washington, and who knows if it will have any impact, or I can reduce my carbon footprint right here."

I ask Bill to tell me of a moment when it came to him that the couple made the right decision, when it all felt really good. Maybe not a big high profile moment, but one of those subtle, passing moments of everydayness when the realization struck.

"When we first moved to Cadillac, we had bought this place, but we had to fix up the house before we could move in, so we were renting two miles away. Our shop was here, and our hay was here, but our animals were at the rental place. It was a chore, bringing the hay to the house by horse all the time.

"And one night," he continues, "when the work day was done, we were going home with some hay, and it was zero degrees, and the boys were snuggled in for warmth, I remember saying to the boys, you could be living in Novi or Livonia and driving to a mall or a drugstore, but instead you are driving down this road, and you have a purpose for doing it. Not just a hobby or an event or recreation, but a purpose that is actually part of your life.

Do you know how lucky you are for that?"

Chapter 5

AMISH COURT CASES/LEGAL NEWS

AMISH DOCKET

It's probably not a coincidence that some of the most important court cases involving the Amish originated in states that typically aren't associated with them. Wisconsin, back in the 1960s, had a very small Amish population. That has now changed. Minnesota also has traditionally not had a large Amish population, but one of the most important cases involving the orange safety emblem on the back of buggies was litigated there. Whenever a "new" culture moves into an unfamiliar area, there are bound to be clashes and conflict, some of which end up in court. New York State has not traditionally been a bastion of Amish culture and that has caused some clashes in Upstate New York between the ultraconservative Swartzentruber Amish their beliefs vs. local township building code ordinances.

Let's take a look at some notable court cases involving the Amish. Reprinted are the actual cases, commentary by Amish Cook editor Kevin Williams is interspersed throughout in bold-faced type.

YODER VS. WISCONSIN

Wisconsin - The Badger State

BACKGROUND: In 1969, Jonas Yoder and Wallace Miller, both members of the Old Order Amish religion, and Adin Yutzy, a member of the Conservative Amish Mennonite Church, were prosecuted under a

Wisconsin law that required all children to attend public schools until age 16. The three parents refused to send their children to such schools after the eighth grade, arguing that high school attendance was contrary to their religious beliefs. Three years later the case eventually made its way to the Supreme Court of the United States. Let's look at the case:

CHIEF JUSTICE BURGER delivered the opinion of the Court.

For the reasons hereafter stated we affirm the judgment of the Supreme Court of Wisconsin. *(The Wisconsin Supreme Court sided with the Amish but the state appealed the matter to the US Supreme Court)*

Respondents Jonas Yoder and Wallace Miller are members of the Old Order Amish religion, and respondent Adin Yutzy is a member of the Conservative Amish Mennonite Church. They and their families are residents of Green County, Wisconsin *(this is a rural county in the southern part of the state which still has an Amish population today)* Wisconsin's compulsory school-attendance law required them to cause their children to attend public or private school until reaching age 16 but the respondents declined to send their children, ages 14 and 15, to public school after they completed the eighth grade. The children were not enrolled in any private school, or within any recognized exception to the compulsory-attendance law, and they are conceded to be subject to the Wisconsin statute.

On complaint of the school district administrator for the public schools, respondents were charged, tried, and convicted of violating the compulsory-attendance law in Green County Court and were fined the sum of $5 each *(in 2010 dollars, adjusted for inflation, that fee would equal to about $27...so this was truly a battle of principle, not price!)* Respondents defended on the ground that the application of the compulsory-attendance law violated their rights under the First and Fourteenth Amendments. The trial testimony showed that respondents believed, in accordance with the tenets of Old Order Amish communities generally, that their children's attendance at high school, public or private, was contrary to the Amish religion and way of life. They believed that by sending their children to high school, they would not only expose themselves to the danger of the censure of the church community, but, as found by the county court, also endanger their own salvation and that of their children. The State stipulated that respondents' religious beliefs were sincere. **(This is a key part of the case: as school districts were consolidating in the 1960s and 1970s, religion's influence in the schools was on the wane, and technology was creeping in, the Amish saw education much beyond the eighth grade as a real threat. And while this factor isn't mentioned in the official transcripts, you have to believe that the "times" also played a role...the "hippie" and anti-war movement was at its zenith, the drug culture was more widespread, the Amish were probably also, in part, reacting to that)**

In support of their position, respondents presented as expert witnesses scholars on religion and education whose testimony is uncontradicted. They expressed their opinions on the relationship of the Amish belief concerning school attendance to the more general tenets of their religion, and described the impact that compulsory high school attendance could have on the continued survival of Amish communities as they exist in the United States today. The history of the Amish sect was given in some detail, beginning with the Swiss Anabaptists of the 16th century who rejected institutionalized churches and sought to return to the early, simple, Christian life de-emphasizing material success, rejecting the competitive spirit, and seeking to insulate themselves from the modern world. As a result of their common heritage, Old Order Amish communities today are characterized by a fundamental belief that salvation requires life in a church community separate and apart from the world and worldly influence. This concept of life aloof from the world and its values is central to their faith.

A related feature of Old Order Amish communities is their devotion to a life in harmony with nature and the soil, as exemplified by the simple life of the early Christian era that continued in America during much of our early national life. Amish beliefs require members of the community to make their living by farming or closely related activities. Broadly speaking, the Old Order Amish religion pervades and determines the entire mode of life of its adherents.

Amish objection to formal education beyond the eighth grade is firmly grounded in these central religious concepts. They object to the high school, and higher education generally, because the values they teach are in marked variance with Amish values and the Amish way of life; they view secondary school education as an impermissible exposure of their children to a "worldly" influence in conflict with their beliefs. The high school tends to emphasize intellectual and scientific accomplishments, self-distinction, competitiveness, worldly success, and social life with other students. Amish society emphasizes informal learning-through-doing; a life of "goodness," rather than a life of intellect; wisdom, rather than technical knowledge; community welfare, rather than competition; and separation from, rather than integration with, contemporary worldly society.

Formal high school education beyond the eighth grade is contrary to Amish beliefs, not only because it places Amish children in an environment hostile to Amish beliefs with increasing emphasis on competition in class work and sports and with pressure to conform to the styles, manners, and ways of the peer group, but also because it takes them away from their community, physically and emotionally, during the crucial and formative adolescent period of life. During this period, the children must acquire Amish attitudes favoring manual work and self-reliance and the specific skills needed to perform the adult role of an Amish farmer or housewife.

(This ruling seems to stand up very well over time, because this opinion was written, of course, long before the internet, cell phones, and other once unthinkable technologies that the Amish have generally been opposed to)

Once a child has learned basic reading, writing, and elementary mathematics, these traits, skills, and attitudes admittedly fall within the category of those best learned through example and "doing" rather than in a classroom. And, at this time in life, the Amish child must also grow in his faith and his relationship to the Amish community if he is to be prepared to accept the heavy obligations imposed by adult baptism. In short, high school attendance with teachers who are not of the Amish faith — and may even be hostile to it — interposes a serious barrier to the integration of the Amish child into the Amish religious community. Dr. John Hostetler, one of the experts on Amish society, testified that the modern high school is not equipped, in curriculum or social environment, to impart the values promoted by Amish society.

The Amish do not object to elementary education through the first eight grades as a general proposition because they agree that their children must have basic skills in the "three R's" in order to read the Bible, to be good farmers and citizens, and to be able to deal with non-Amish people when necessary in the course of daily affairs. They view such a basic education as acceptable because it does not significantly expose their children to worldly values or interfere with their development in the Amish community during the crucial adolescent period. While Amish accept compulsory elementary education generally, wherever possible they have established their own elementary schools in many respects like the small local schools of the past.

(Amish-run parochial schools are often so soundly steeped in the basics of "reading, writing, and arithmetic," that some Amish 8th graders could pass a GED without ever spending a day in high school)

In the Amish belief higher learning tends to develop values they reject as influences that alienate man from God.

(Key testimony below!)

On the basis of such considerations, Dr. Hostetler testified that compulsory high school attendance could not only result in great psychological harm to Amish children, because of the conflicts it would produce, but would also, in his opinion, ultimately result in the destruction of the Old Order Amish church community as it exists in the United States today.

The testimony of Dr. Donald A. Erickson, an expert witness on education, also showed that the Amish succeed in preparing their high school age children to be productive members of the Amish community. He described their system of learning through doing the skills directly relevant to their adult roles in the Amish community as "ideal" and perhaps superior to ordinary high school education. The evidence also showed that the Amish have an excellent record as law-abiding and generally self-sufficient members of society....

The following paragraphs can amount to a bit of a snore, but for policy wonks it is good stuff and in order to understand the importance of the opinion and the reasoning behind it, the whole opinion is being printed here.

There is no doubt as to the power of a State, having a high responsibility for education of its citizens, to impose reasonable regulations for the control and duration of basic education. Providing public schools ranks at the very apex of the function of a State. Yet even this paramount responsibility was, in *Pierce*, made to yield to the right of parents to provide an equivalent education in a privately operated system. There the Court held that Oregon's statute compelling attendance in a public school from age eight to age 16 unreasonably interfered with the interest of parents in directing the rearing of their offspring, including their education in church-operated schools. As that case suggests, the values of parental direction of the religious upbringing and education of their children in their early and formative years have a high place in our society. Thus, a State's interest in universal education, however highly we rank it, is not totally free from a balancing process when it impinges on fundamental rights and interests, such as those specifically protected by the Free Exercise Clause of the First Amendment, and the traditional interest of parents with respect to the religious upbringing of their children so long as they "prepare [them] for additional obligations." It follows that in order for Wisconsin to compel school attendance beyond the eighth grade against a claim that such attendance interferes with the practice of a legitimate religious belief, it must appear either that the State does not deny the free exercise of religious belief by its requirement, or that there is a state interest of sufficient magnitude to override the interest claiming protection under the Free Exercise Clause.... The essence of all that has been said and written on the subject is that only those interests of the highest order and those not otherwise served can overbalance legitimate claims to the free exercise of religion. We can accept it as settled, therefore, that, however strong the State's interest in universal compulsory education, it is by no means absolute to the exclusion or subordination of all other interests.

We come then to the quality of the claims of the respondents concerning the alleged encroachment of Wisconsin's compulsory school-attendance statute on their rights and the rights of their children to the free exercise of the religious beliefs they and their forebears have adhered to for almost three centuries. In evaluating those claims we must be careful to determine whether the Amish religious faith and their mode of life are, as they claim, inseparable and interdependent. A way of life, however virtuous and admirable, may not be interposed as a barrier to reasonable state regulation of education if it is based on purely secular considerations; to have the protection of the Religion Clauses, the claims must be rooted in religious belief. Although a determination of what is a "religious" belief or practice entitled to constitutional protection may present a most delicate question, the very concept of ordered liberty precludes allowing every person to make his own standards on matters of conduct in which society as a whole has important interests. Thus, if the Amish asserted their claims because of their subjective evaluation and rejection of the contemporary secular values accepted by the majority, much as Thoreau rejected the social values of his time and isolated himself at Walden Pond, their claims would not rest on a religious basis. Thoreau's choice was philosophical and personal rather than religious, and such belief does not rise to the demands of the Religion Clauses.

Giving no weight to such secular considerations, however, we see that the record in this case abundantly supports the claim that the traditional way of life of the Amish is not merely a matter of personal preference, but one of deep religious conviction, shared by an organized group, and intimately related to daily living....

The conclusion is inescapable that secondary schooling, by exposing Amish children to worldly influences in terms of attitudes, goals, and values contrary to beliefs, and by substantially interfering with the religious development of the Amish child and his integration into the way of life of the Amish faith community at the crucial adolescent stage of development, contravenes the basic religious tenets and practice of the Amish faith, both as to the parent and the child.

The impact of the compulsory-attendance law on respondents' practice of the Amish religion is not only severe, but inescapable, for the Wisconsin law affirmatively compels them, under threat of criminal sanction, to perform acts undeniably at odds with fundamental tenets of their religious beliefs. As the record shows, compulsory school attendance to age 16 for Amish children carries with it a very real threat of undermining the Amish community and religious practice as they exist today; they must either abandon belief and be assimilated into society at large, or be forced to migrate to some other and more tolerant region.

In sum, the unchallenged testimony of acknowledged experts in education and religious history, almost 300 years of consistent practice, and strong evidence of a sustained faith pervading and regulating respondents' entire mode of life support the claim that enforcement of the State's requirement of compulsory formal education after the eighth grade would gravely endanger if not destroy the free exercise of respondents' religious beliefs.

Neither the findings of the trial court nor the Amish claims as to the nature of their faith are challenged in this Court by the State of Wisconsin. Its position is that the State's interest in universal compulsory formal secondary education to age 16 is so great that it is paramount to the undisputed claims of respondents that their mode of preparing their youth for Amish life, after the traditional elementary education, is an essential part of their religious belief and practice....Nor can this case be disposed of on the grounds that Wisconsin's requirement for school attendance to age 16 applies uniformly to all citizens of the State and does not, on its face, discriminate against religions or a particular religion, or that it is motivated by legitimate secular concerns. A regulation neutral on its face may, in its application, nonetheless offend the constitutional requirement for governmental neutrality if it unduly burdens the free exercise of religion.

The State advances two primary arguments in support of its system of compulsory education. It notes, as Thomas Jefferson pointed out early in our history, that some degree of education is necessary to prepare citizens to participate effectively and intelligently in our open political system if we are to preserve freedom and independence. Further, education prepares individuals to be self-reliant and self-sufficient participants in society. We accept these propositions.

However, the evidence adduced by the Amish in this case is persuasively to the effect that an additional one or two years of formal high school for Amish children in place of their long-established program of informal vocational education would do little to serve those interests. Respondents' experts testified at trial, without challenge, that the value of all education must be assessed in terms of its capacity to prepare the child for life. It is one thing to say that compulsory education for a year or two beyond the eighth grade may be necessary when its goal is the preparation of the child for life in modern society as the majority live, but it is quite another if the goal of education be viewed as the preparation of the child for life in the separated agrarian community that is the keystone of the Amish faith.

The State attacks respondents' position as one fostering "ignorance" from which the child must be protected by the State. No one can question the State's duty to protect children from ignorance but this argument does not square with the facts disclosed in the record. Whatever their idiosyncrasies as seen by the majority, this record strongly shows that the Amish community has been a highly successful social unit within our society, even if apart from the conventional "mainstream." Its members are productive and very law-abiding members of society; they reject public welfare in any of its usual modern forms.

The State, however, supports its interest in providing an additional one or two years of compulsory high school education to Amish children because of the possibility that some such children will choose to leave the Amish community, and that if this occurs they will be ill-equipped for life. The State argues that if Amish children leave their church they should not be in the position of making their way in the world without the education available in the one or two additional years the State requires. However, on this record, that argument is highly speculative. There is no specific evidence of the loss of Amish adherents by attrition, nor is there any showing that upon leaving the Amish community Amish children, with their practical agricultural training and habits of industry and self-reliance, would become burdens on society because of educational short-comings.

Finally, the State, on authority of *Prince* v. *Massachusetts*, argues that a decision exempting Amish children from the State's requirement fails to recognize the substantive right of the Amish child to a secondary education, and fails to give due regard to the power of the State as *parens patriae* to extend the benefit of secondary education to children regardless of the wishes of their parents.

This case, of course, is not one in which any harm to the physical or mental health of the child or to the public safety, peace, order, or welfare has been demonstrated or may be properly inferred. The record is to the contrary, and any reliance on that theory would find no support in the evidence.

Contrary to the suggestion of the dissenting opinion of MR. JUSTICE DOUGLAS, our holding today in no degree depends on the assertion of the religious interest of the child as contrasted with that of the parents. It is the parents who are subject to prosecution here for failing to cause their children to attend school, and it is their right of free exercise, not that of their children, that must determine Wisconsin's power to impose criminal penalties on the parent. The dissent argues that a child who expresses a desire to attend public high school in conflict with the wishes of his parents should not be prevented from doing so. There is no reason for the Court to consider that point since it is not an issue in the case. The children are not parties to this litigation. The State has at no point tried this case on the theory that respondents were preventing their children from attending school against their expressed desires, and indeed the record is to the contrary. The State's position from the outset has been that it is empowered to apply its compulsory-attendance law to Amish parents in the same manner as to other parents — that is, without regard to the wishes of the child. That is the claim we reject today.

Our holding in no way determines the proper resolution of possible competing interests of parents, children, and the State in an appropriate state court proceeding in which the power of the State is asserted on the theory that Amish parents are preventing their minor children from attending high school despite their expressed desires to the contrary....

JUSTICE DOUGLAS, dissenting in part.

Justice Douglas makes, in the opinion of this editor, some extremely compelling arguments. The majority of the Court felt that the compulsory education would destroy the Amish CHURCH. Justice Douglas, however, looked at how depriving education impacts the INDIVIDUAL. This case was a tricky one and I am glad I wasn't one of those Supreme Court case justices. On one hand, you had the interests in preserving the culture as a whole pitted against individual rights.

I agree with the Court that the religious scruples of the Amish are opposed to the education of their children beyond the grade schools, yet I disagree with the Court's conclusion that the matter is within the dispensation of parents alone. The Court's analysis assumes that the only interests at stake in the case are those of the Amish parents on the one hand, and those of the State on the other. The difficulty with this approach is that, despite the Court's claim, the parents are seeking to vindicate not only their own free exercise claims, but also those of their high-school-age children....

Recent cases, however, have clearly held that the children themselves have constitutionally protectable interests. These children are "persons" within the meaning of the Bill of Rights. We have so held over and over again.

On this important and vital matter of education, I think the children should be entitled to be heard. While the parents, absent dissent, normally speak for the entire family, the education of the child is a matter on which the child will often have decided views. He may want to be a pianist or an astronaut or an oceanographer. To do so he will have to break from the Amish tradition.

It is the future of the student, not the future of the parents, that is imperiled by today's decision. If a parent keeps his child out of school beyond the grade school, then the child will be forever barred from entry into the new and amazing world of diversity that we have today. The child may decide that that is the preferred course, or he may rebel. It is the student's judgment, not his parents,' that is essential if we are to give full meaning to what we have said about the Bill of Rights and of the right of students to be masters of their own destiny. If he is harnessed to the Amish way of life by those in authority over him and if his education is truncated, his entire life may be stunted and deformed. The child, therefore, should be given an opportunity to be heard before the State gives the exemption which we honor today.

The views of the two children in question were not canvassed by the Wisconsin courts. The matter should be explicitly reserved so that new hearings can be held on remand of the case.

Justice Burger's opinion stood and the Amish have slowly shifted towards their own parochial schools ever since this 1972 case. Some Amish also home-school their children while others still attend public schools, but they tend to be smaller, more rural districts.

MINNESOTA V. HERSHBERGER

Amish residents were given traffic citations for failing to display slow-moving vehicle symbols on their buggies. The case was before the Minnesota Supreme Court on remand from the United States Supreme Court to be considered in light of the U.S. Supreme Court's holding in *Employment Div., Dep't of Human Resources of Oregon v. Smith*, 110 S. Ct. 1595 (1990). In *Smith*, the U.S. Supreme Court held that a law of general application, one that is not intended to regulate religious belief or

conduct, is not invalid if the law incidentally infringes on religious practices (e.g., state can prohibit use of peyote despite the fact that the drug is used during some Native American religious ceremonies).

The Amish alleged that their religious beliefs prohibited them from displaying the symbols required by the statute that they were cited for violating. The Minnesota Supreme Court recognized "that individual liberties under the state constitution may deserve greater protection than those under the broadly worded federal constitution." It concluded that regardless of the effect of the *Smith* decision, the state had failed to show that there was not a less-restrictive alternative to displaying the slow-moving vehicle symbols. Such a showing is required under the Minnesota Constitution in light of the conclusion that the defendant's reason for disobeying the statute was a sincere religious belief. The charges against the Amish for disobeying the statute were dismissed.

State v. Hershberger, 462 N.W.2d 393 (Minn. 1990)

Amish families from Ohio began to arrive in Fillmore County, Minnesota in 1973-74. As a religious community, they adopted a simple lifestyle, traveling by horse and buggy. At first, there were few problems with the Minnesota law requiring an orange and red triangular slow-moving vehicle sign to be displayed on buggies and wagons. Younger Amish, conscious of their position as newcomers and anxious to fit into their new community, tended to use the required sign. Some Amish preferred to display a black triangle outlined in white as a compromise. Others refused to use any sign. They believed the bright colors of the sign and the symbol itself would put their faith in "worldly symbols" rather than in God. Instead, they outlined their buggies with silver reflective tape. If stopped and tagged, Amish drivers usually pled not guilty. Routinely, they were found guilty and then paid the fines.

Concerns were raised by people living in the area. Occasional accidents involving slow-moving vehicles showed the need for such signs to protect public safety. In 1986, Minnesota law was changed to allow the black triangle with a white outline. Many Amish agreed to this compromise. But in 1987, when the law was changed again to require the orange triangle to always be carried in the wagon and used at night or in poor weather, the conflict grew.

Amish who refused to carry the sign began to be ticketed, fined, and sentenced to community service or jail time. Initial fines were $20 - $22, and first time jail sentences were seven days. Jail sentences would not have to be served if there were no additional tags within six months. Soon, repeat offenders began to appear back in court within the six-month period, refused to pay fines, and were required to serve time in jail.

In December 1988, Mr. Hershberger and thirteen others appeared before a judge for violation of the sign law. They asked the court to dismiss the traffic citations explaining their refusal to display the sign was based on their sincere religious beliefs and that the sign law punished them for their beliefs through fines and jail time. They wanted to practice their religion without interference from government as guaranteed in the First Amendment. They believed the law should allow an alternative that would not violate their religion - the use of silver reflective tape.

The judge refused to dismiss the citations, pointing out that the Amish community was divided on whether or not their religion prohibits display of the sign. Because of this, it did not appear to the judge that the religious belief was sincere. The judge also felt that highway safety was a more important consideration. However, the judge did ask the Minnesota Court of Appeals to consider the constitutional questions, which were then forwarded to the Minnesota Supreme Court. The Minnesota Supreme Court found that the law violated the Free Exercise Clause of the U.S. Constitution. As a result, the trial court's decision to refuse to dismiss the charges was set aside and all charges against the Amish were dismissed.

The State appealed to the U.S. Supreme Court. The U.S. Supreme Court agreed to consider the case. At the same time, the court was considering a free exercise of religion case arising out of religious use of peyote. In this case, *Employment Division, Department of Human Resources of Oregon v. Smith* (1990), the Supreme Court significantly changed First Amendment free exercise analysis. The court held that a law of general application, which does not intend to regulate religious belief or conduct, is not invalid because the law incidentally infringes on religious practices.

The U.S. Supreme Court remanded (sent back) the *Hershberger* case to the Minnesota Supreme Court for reconsideration, applying the new standards decided under *Smith*. In addition to the *Smith* decision interpreting the U.S. Supreme Court, the Minnesota Court also had to consider the protections offered by Article 1, Section 16 of the Minnesota Constitution.

Issue

Does Minnesota law requiring the slow-moving vehicle sign violate the rights of the Amish to free exercise of religion guaranteed in the Minnesota Constitution and the U.S. Constitution?

Points of Law

Under Article I, Section 16 of the Minnesota Constitution, individuals are provided the following protections.

> **Freedom of conscience; no preference to be given to any religious establishment or mode of worship.** *The enumeration of rights in this constitution shall not deny or impair others retained by and inherent in the people. The right of every man to worship God according to the dictates of his own conscience shall never be infringed; nor shall any man be compelled to attend, erect or support any place of worship, or to maintain any religious or ecclesiastical ministry, against his consent; nor shall any control of or interference with the rights of conscience be permitted, or any preference be given by law to any religious establishment or mode of worship; but the liberty of conscience hereby secured shall not be so construed as to excuse acts of*

licentiousness or justify practices inconsistent with the peace or safety of the state, nor shall any money be drawn from the treasury for the benefit of any religious societies or religious or theological seminaries.

The First Amendment to the U.S. Constitution reads, "Congress shall make no law respecting an establishment of religion, or prohibiting the free exercise thereof. . . ." The amendment's guarantee of freedom of religion contains two parts: (1) the establishment clause, and (2) the free exercise clause.

Under the establishment clause, the state may not treat one religion more favorably than others so as to make it appear that the government is supporting that religion as the state-approved religion. The clause has also been interpreted to forbid government from aiding religion in general over non-religion.

Under the free exercise clause, the state may not restrict the free exercise of religious beliefs either directly or by imposing burdensome conditions on these beliefs.

There is a balance that must be struck between the two clauses. In protecting the free exercise of one religion, it is easy for the government to seem to be favoring (establishing) that religion. For example, if it makes an exception and says that people whose religious beliefs prohibit violence do not have to be soldiers, people with other beliefs might think the government is treating the first religion more favorably.

As with other First Amendment freedoms, the Constitution's protection of religious beliefs must be balanced against the important needs of society as a whole. That means that the importance of a religious activity to a particular religion must be balanced against the harm to society that the activity can cause. For instance, although public dancing with poisonous snakes may be important to a religious group, the danger that such an activity poses to the public could allow the state to prevent it without running afoul of the free exercise clause.

The Court's Decision

In comparing the language of the Minnesota Constitution with the language of the First Amendment to the U.S. Constitution which says

"Congress shall make no law respecting an establishment of religion, or prohibiting the free exercise of...," the Court said "This language [the Minnesota Constitution] is of a distinctively stronger character than the federal counterpart." Accordingly, government actions that may not constitute an outright prohibition on religious practices (thus not violating the First Amendment) could nonetheless infringe on or interfere with those practices, violating the Minnesota Constitution. The state Bill of Rights expressly grants affirmative rights in the area of religious worship while the corresponding federal provision simply attempts to restrain governmental action.

The Minnesota Supreme Court, in interpreting the protections of the Minnesota Constitution, chose to use the standards that had been used by the U.S. Supreme Court prior to *Smith*: that the state must demonstrate (1) a compelling state interest in the goal of the law and (2) that there is no less restrictive alternative to the action required or prohibited by the law.

"Only the government's interest in peace or safety or against acts of licentiousness will excuse an imposition on religious freedom under the Minnesota Constitution. . . Rather than a blanket denial of a religious exemption whenever public safety is involved, only religious practices found to be inconsistent with public safety are denied an exemption. By juxtaposing individual rights of conscience with the interest of the state in public safety, this provision invites the court to balance competing values in a manner that the compelling state interest test . . .articulates: once a claimant has demonstrated a sincere religious belief intended to be protected by Section 16, the state should be required to demonstrate that public safety cannot be achieved by proposed alternative means."

The Court ruled that the state failed to demonstrate that the alternative signs did not protect public safety, and therefore the application of the Minnesota law to the Amish defendants violated their freedom of conscience rights protected by the Minnesota Constitution.

DOWN THE TOILET

Throughout 2008- 2009 a small group of Swartzentruber Amish made news in Pennsylvania for improper disposal of human waste. An Amish school-house was deemed in violation of local health codes for collecting potty sewage in buckets and then just spreading it on surrounding fields. A few Swartzentruber Amish homes in the area were also targeted by authorities for the same violations. The issue came to a head when one of the Amish homes and the school was ordered padlocked. As of 2010, the homes and the school are still padlocked and the issues is dragging through the courts.

Here is a transcript of an amishcookonline interview with Dave Beyer one of the attorneys representing the Amish.

AMISHCOOKONLINE: How did you become involved in this case?

DAVE BEYER: I am primarily a criminal defense attorney and I was visiting one of my clients in the Cambria County prison when I noticed there were some Amish people sitting in the waiting area. I knew one of their church members had been incarcerated because it had made local news. I was visiting a client in jail and saw the Amish people there and I just said: "This isn't right, these are good, caring, loving people and for them to be incarcerated over something as ridiculous as this is just crazy." I knew I had become involved

AMISHCOOKONLINE: Had you had much prior experience with the Amish?

DAVE BEYER: No, I hadn't. Being in Pennsylvania, I was always aware of and respected their way of life. I think they have the right take on a lot of things. I respect their peaceful living, I respect their peaceful living, way they live, and their religion, I think our world would be a lot better off if we took lessons from them.

AMISHCOOKONLINE: It is just a handful of Swartzentrubers being targeted, but there is a larger group, so the question that often comes up: are the other Swartzentrubers complying and is it just a handful of people that aren't?

BEYER: This sect strongly feels that this outhouse issue, this human waste issues is something they can't break from. They feel strongly that their religious beliefs don't allow them to modernize their facilities and they feel equally strongly that they aren't harming anyone. And that, quite frankly, is something I agree with them. These people live on 50,100, or 150 acre farms, we are not talking about a lot of people, not hundreds people, there are a handful. There is no way anyone can convince me that they are endangering anyone else's health, safety or welfare. No way. The amount of human waste we are talking about is insignificant. And I agree with them that whenever they plow this waste into their fields in the middle of a 150 acre field no one is going to be harmed, neighbors are not going to be harmed, it is not going to end up in well water. They'll mix the waste with cow manure and plow it into the fields and the sun will evaporate the rest. They have been living this way for hundreds of years. There is no data to support that these people pose a harm. I don't know why the municipality decided to pick on these people. I think this is an overly aggressive municipality infringing on these people's rights. I do feel this is a religious issue. The local judge has determined it is not a religious issue and I disagree.

AMISHCOOKONLINE: Why don't they just rent a port-a-potty for a few months at the school while they litigate this at least so they can keep the school open?

BEYER: One of my goals when I got involved I was trying to find a middle ground to appease everyone. I called a place about renting a port-o-potty, but the Amish had advised me that this was unacceptable. The Amish advised me that that was unacceptable, that a port-o-potty was considered a modern convenience. They acknowledge if they are traveling somewhere they will use those sort of facilities, but they cannot allow a port-o-potty to be placed on their property. They have held fast that it infringes on their beliefs.

AMISHCOOKONLINE: So where does this go from here?

BEYER: The case may go to Superior Court of even the Supreme Court. In other cases involving the Amish like the landmark school case (Yoder vs. Wisconsin) the courts have to apply a "balancing of interests" standard. The same thing needs to be done here. "Is it a sincere belief?" The Courts have to make sure it is a sincere belief. I believe the Amish would pass that part of the test. Then they have to ask "does the law interfere with their religious beliefs." Clearly, it does. Then they need to balance the interest of the commonwealth vs. religious freedom and then make a decision. But even if the Amish decide to litigate this it would take years to resolve.

AMISHCOOKONLINE: So what do we do in the meantime?

The judge has bent has far as he can bend without breaking any laws. He proposed a holding tank underneath the outhouse, agreed to allow a port-o-potty, agreed to open the barns so they could get their crops in and take care of their livestock. He is looking for the Amish to come somewhere and meet them in the middle. So far that is not happening.

Chapter 6

RECIPES FOR FOOD AND HOME

RECESSION AND DEPRESSION DISHES

The Amish, like everyone else, are slowly evolving in their culinary tastes. While working on our recently completed book, Lovina wrote about how her mother used to eat the lungs and brains of hogs after slaughtering them. Scrambled eggs and brains was a favorite. While Lovina's mother loved the dish, Lovina just doesn't find it too appetizing. This is a very typical generational shift in taste.

The Amish are very inventive when it comes to culinary matters, but these days their inventiveness is more likely trained on taming ethnic foods like tacos, salsa, pizzas, and finding unique ways to use prepared foods like cream of mushroom soup and Jello. In earlier times, even just a generation or two ago, the culinary experiences of the Amish were forged by tough times: their journey to the New World and surviving the Great Depression. The Amish became experts at scratching meals out of virtually nothing. A few "meals" that were once popular among the Amish but are now disappearing from the menus of a younger generation:

COFFEE SOUP: Lovina's mother used to enjoy having this as did her grandmother. The common breakfast meal was nothing more than a mug filled with crumbled crackers or bread cubes and then topped off with hot, fresh coffee. Lovina's husband Joe still enjoys this, but it's less commonly found in Amish homes today.

COLD MILK SOUP: This sounds a bit more palatable than "coffee soup." This "meal" would be enjoyed on warm summer evenings. This dish consists of no more than a bowl filled with cold milk, freshly picked wild berries and a sprinkling of sugar.

BROWN FLOUR SOUP: A pasty concoction of flour and milk that would serve as supper during lean times.

RIVVEL SOUP: just bits of dough dropped in boiling broth.

VINEGAR PIE: Gross name, great pie!!! Citrus was in short supply during the Great Depression and other tight times...this pie actually comes out tasting like a lemon pie.

VINEGAR PIE

1/2 c. butter, softened
2 tbsp. cider vinegar
1 (8 inch) unbaked pie shell
3 eggs
1 tsp. vanilla
1 1/4 c. sugar

Cream butter and sugar until light and fluffy. Add eggs, vinegar, and vanilla. Pour into unbaked pie shell. Bake at 350 for 45 minutes or until inserted knife comes out clean.

FRIENDSHIP BREAD

Elizabeth had only been writing her column for a few weeks in the fall of 1991 when the first letters - the letters about Amish Friendship Bread - began coming. I'm a journalist, not a cook, so I guess it is not surprising that I had never heard of that. Puzzled by the passion behind this recipe, I took the letters up to Elizabeth. She, too, was mystified by it. She had never made "Amish Friendship Bread," and neither had anyone else in her community.

Elizabeth researched the topic and eventually found some Amish women in Ohio who were very familiar with the recipe. That's where she got the recipe, and over the years since those first letters came, she's become very familiar with it. The letters, though, still keep coming. People are always requesting this recipe. So, without further delay, here is that recipe. There are some tips and background after the recipe.

AMISH FRIENDSHIP BREAD

By Elizabeth Coblentz

PART I (Instructions for the sourdough starter):

3 1/2 cups of bread flour
1 tablespoon of sugar
1 package of dry, active yeast
2 cups of warm water

Combine flour, sugar, and undissolved yeast into a large bowl. Gradually add warm water to dry ingredients. Beat until smooth. Cover with transparent wrap and let stand in a warm place for two days.

PART II

1 cup of starter
1 cup of flour
1 1/2 teaspoons of baking powder
1 cup of sugar
3 eggs
1 cup of milk
2 teaspoons of cinnamon
1 cup of flour
1 teaspoon of vanilla
1 cup of sugar
1/2 teaspoons of salt
1 cup of milk
1/2 teaspoon of soda
2/3 cup of oil
1 large box of vanilla instant pudding
2 cups of flour
1 cup of chopped nuts (optional)
1/2 cups of sugar

Directions:

- **Day 1:** Do nothing to the starter.
- **Day 2,3,4:** Stir starter with a wooden spoon
- **Day 5:** Add one cup of flour, 1 cup of sugar, 1 cup of milk. Stir with wooden spoon. Re-cover the mixture and set in a warm place.
- **Day 6,7,8,9:** Stir with a wooden spoon and re-cover.
- **Day 10:** Add 1 cup of flour, 1 cup of sugar, 1 cup of milk, stir.

Divide into three containers (1 cup each) and give to three friends with these instructions:

To remainder: add 2/3 cup of oil, 2 cups of flour, 3 eggs, 2 teaspoons of cinnamon, 1 teaspoons of vanilla, 1/2 teaspoon of salt, and 1/2 teaspoon of soda. Add one large box of instant vanilla pudding mix and one cup of nuts. Pour into two well-greased and floured loaf pans and bake 40 to 50 minutes at 350. Watch towards the end of baking time and cover with foil to prevent burning. Also, test for doneness with a toothpick so it does not get too well done. Cool in pans for 10 minutes and then remove. Do not use a metal spoon. Do not refrigerate. Cover loosely. You can also bake this in a bundt pan.

BACKGROUND: Amish lore has several stories for the origins of this popular, sweet-tasting bread. One is that on an Amish woman's wedding day, the mother would supply her daughter with some sourdough starter of her own, and the young bride would begin making the bread for her own family. The bread then gets passed from generation to generation. This practice still exists in some remote Amish communities, but it seems to have died out among most. Others suggest that this was simply a fun bread to make during those cold winter nights and that it became popular as a gift to shut-ins or the infirmed.

STARTER TIPS: Do not use self-rising flour. When you cover the starter, If you use foil, don't let the foil fall into the starter. Let starter sit in a quiet place, away from drafts or hot breezes. You'll know the starter (some call it's completed form, a "sponge") is done when:

- it tastes "good"
- the texture is creamy (not "gritty")
- there is no "flour taste"
  - the sponge is pourable and will flow back together slowly on the back of a spoon.

AMISH COOK CLASSICS

WASHDAY CASSEROLE

3 pounds of hamburger
3 onions, chopped
3 cups of potatoes, peeled and diced
3 cups of celery, diced
3 cups of cooked spaghetti
2 (10 3/4 ounce) cans of cream of mushroom soup
9 slices of bacon
1 (32 ounce) quart of tomato juice
1 pound of cheddar cheese, grated

Brown crumbled hamburger and onions in a pan. Drain and pour hamburger mix into large casserole or deep 9x13 inch baking pan. Add potatoes, celery, and spaghetti to casserole and mix lightly with hamburger. Pour mushroom soup on top and spread evenly. Fry bacon and lay on top. Pour tomato juice over this. Add cheese over that. Bake 1 1/2 hours in 350 degree oven. Serves 10 to 12.

AUNT HILTY'S CINNAMON ROLLS

These rolls go good around here, especially for breakfast. Everyone seems to enjoy them.

1 1/2 cups milk
2 teaspoons salt
1/2 cup sugar
1/2 cup butter
2 packages of dry, active yeast
1/2 cup warm water
6 cups flour
3 eggs

Scald 1 1/2 cups milk. Add two teaspoons of salt, 1/2 cup sugar, and 1/2 cup butter or margarine. Add two packages of yeast to 1/2 cup of warm water and let stand five minutes. Add to above mixture. Add three beaten eggs and then three cups of flour. Mix. Add three cups more flour. Let raise to double bulk. Roll out and spread with melted margarine. Sprinkle brown sugar on top and then cinnamon. Roll-up. Cut up about 3/4 to one inch width. Let rise. Bake in hot oven (about 350), five to seven minutes. Frosting can be added.

HOMEMADE BUTTERMILK PIE

Pat A Pan Pie Crust (page XXX)

1/2 cup butter, softened
1 cup fresh buttermilk
3 large eggs
1 1/2 cups sugar
1 tablespoon flour
1 teaspoon of nutmeg

Preheat oven to 350. Roll the disk of pie dough out to a 1/8 inch thickness on a floured surface. Fit the dough into a 9 inch pie pan. Trim any overhang to 1 inch. Fold the dough under and crimp the edges. In a large bowl beat together butter, buttermilk, eggs, sugar, and flour with a whisk. Pour the filling into the piecrust. Sprinkle with nutmeg. Bake for 35 minutes until the pie turns a golden brown color and butter knife inserted in the center comes out clean.

PEANUT BRITTLE

2 cups of sugar
2 cups of salted peanuts
1 cup of honey
1 tablespoon of butter
1 cup of water

Put sugar, honey, and water into a saucepan. Stir until sugar is dissolved. Cook to 285. Remove from fire or heat. Add butter and peanuts. Stir just enough to mix thoroughly. Pour into very thin sheets of well-greased platter and cool. Break into pieces to serve.

COBLENTZ CHRISTMAS COOKIES

These are a favorite Christmas cookie around here. Make them and the longer they sit, the better they taste.

3 cups of flour
3 tablespoon of milk
1 cup of sugar
2 eggs
1 teaspoon of baking soda
1 teaspoon of cream or tartar
1/2 teaspoon of salt
1 teaspoon of vanilla
1 1/4 cup of butter

Mix dry ingredients. Add remaining ingredients and stir until you get a soft dough. Roll out thinly. Cut in any shape desired. Bake for 375 for about 10 minutes until the cookies are golden brown around the edges. Let cool and decorate as you wish. These cookies taste great for weeks.

SUNDAY POT ROAST

3-4 lb. beef roast (sirloin tip, rump, English cut)
1 tbsp. oil
1/4 c. soy sauce
1 c. coffee
2 bay leaves
1 garlic clove, minced
1/2 tsp. oregano
2 onions, sliced

Sear roast in 1 tablespoon oil on all sides in heavy Dutch oven. Pour sauce over meat. Put half of onions on meat, the other half in sauce. Cover and roast 4–5 hours at 325 degrees.

STICKY CHICKEN

1 chicken cut up
4 tablespoons cooking oil
1/4 cup flour
salt and pepper to taste
butter

Pour about 2 tablespoons oil into skillet. Add a tablespoon of butter if desired. Heat until oil is hot. Coat chicken pieces with flour. Place in hot skillet, sprinkle salt and pepper on pieces and brown on all sides. Remove and place in a 2 quart casserole dish. Do this until all pieces are browned. Rinse skillet with about 1/4 to 1/2 cup water and add to chicken. Place dish, covered into oven at 350 degrees. Bake for 45 minutes to 1 hour. When chicken is done, use drippings to make gravy.

FRIENDSHIP SALAD

1 cup of diced ham
2 cups of cooked macaroni
1 1/2 tablespoon of barbecue sauce
1/4 cup of chopped grated pepper
salt and pepper to taste
1/4 cup of chopped onions
3 tablespoons of mayonnaise
3/4 cup of grated cut celery
1 teaspoon of prepared mustard
1/2 cup of chopped carrots

Combine ham, macaroni, celery, carrots, pepper, and onion. In another bowl, mix in mayonnaise, barbecue sauce, catsup, and mustard. Mix thoroughly and add to other mixture.

MACARONI SALAD

2 cups uncooked elbow macaroni
3 hard-cooked eggs, chopped
1 small onion, chopped
3 stalks celery, chopped
1 small red bell pepper, seeded and chopped
2 tablespoons dill pickle relish
2 cups creamy salad dressing (e.g. Miracle Whip)
3 tablespoons prepared yellow mustard
3/4 cup white sugar
2 1/4 teaspoons white vinegar
1/4 teaspoon salt
3/4 teaspoon celery seed

Bring a pot of lightly salted water to a boil. Add macaroni, and cook for 8 to 10 minutes, until tender. Drain, and set aside to cool.

In a large bowl, stir together the eggs, onion, celery, red pepper, and relish. In a small bowl, stir together the salad dressing, mustard, white sugar, vinegar, salt and celery seed. Pour over the vegetables, and stir in macaroni until well blended. Cover and chill for at least 1 hour before serving.

BANANA CAKE

1/2 cup butter
2 cups all-purpose flour, sifted
1 cup sour milk
1 teaspoon vanilla extract
1 1/2 cups granulated sugar
1 teaspoon baking powder
1 teaspoon baking soda
2 bananas, creamed 2 eggs, beaten

Cream butter and sugar together. Add well beaten eggs. To this mixture, add the sour milk alternately with the sifted flour, baking powder and the baking soda. Add creamed bananas and vanilla extract. Beat with an egg beater. Grease and flour a pan and bake cake at 350 degrees F for about 40 minutes. Cool before removing from pan.

AMISH PUMPKIN BREAD

Autumn gardens feature the arrival of flaming orbs of orange on the end of long, sprawling vines. This is a common sight on Amish farms and in their gardens, as many Amish homemakers have pumpkin patches. The pumpkin is then used in pies, breads, butters, and jellies. Pumpkin is a versatile vegetable that is great way to end the gardening season. Homegrown pumpkin tends to have a lighter color and texture than its store-canned cousins.

Homemade pumpkin bread: we've featured homemade pumpkin bread recipes in the column before, but this is really nutty, delicious, textured bread with wonderful flavor.

3c granulated or raw sugar
1c vegetable oil
4 large eggs, beaten

1 pound fresh or store-bought pumpkin
3 1/2 c flour
2/3 c water
2 tsp baking soda
2 tsp salt
1/2 tsp ground cloves
1 tsp allspice
1 tsp nutmeg
2 tsp cinnamon
1/2 c chopped walnuts

Mix sugar, eggs and oil together. Mix together dry ingredients, add to egg mixture. Add pumpkin and walnuts, and finally water, stirring until mixed. Pour into two greased and floured loaf pans (9x5 inch). Bake 350 degrees for 1 hour til done. Serve with butter, homemade jam

HOMEMADE CARAMEL CORN

Popcorn is an easy, simple snack that brings much enjoyment to Amish families, especially on cold winter nights. Sometimes popcorn is enjoyed plain, other times it's jazzed up with a little butter and salt. And for popcorn with real "pop," caramel corn is a family favorite in many Amish kitchens.

7 quarts plain popped popcorn
2 c. dry roasted peanuts (optional)
2 c. semi sweet chocolate chips (optional)
2 c. brown sugar
1/2 c. light corn syrup
1 teaspoon salt
1 c. margarine or butter
1/2 tsp. baking soda
1 tsp. vanilla extract

Place the popped popcorn into two shallow greased baking pans. You may use roasting pans, jelly roll pans, or disposable roasting pans. If you are using peanuts, add them to the popped corn. Set aside.

Preheat the oven to 250 degrees F (120 degrees C). Combine the brown sugar, corn syrup, butter/margarine and salt in a saucepan. Bring to a boil over medium heat, stirring enough to blend. Once the mixture begins to boil, boil for 5 minutes while stirring constantly.

Remove from heat. Stir in baking soda and vanilla until the mixture is light and foamy. Immediately pour over the popcorn in the pans, and stir until corn is well coated.

Bake for 1 hour, removing the pans, and stirring the corn in the pans every 15 minutes or so. Line the countertop with waxed paper. Dump the corn out onto the waxed paper and separate the pieces. Allow to cool completely, then store in airtight containers or resealable bags

GRANNY SMITH PANCAKES

Apples are used according to their variety. McIntosh apples make a great pie, while the transparent yellow apples are best in a homemade applesauce. The tart, green Granny Smiths really perk up pancakes!

    2 Granny Smith apples, peeled, cored and sliced.
    1 c flour
    1 c milk
    6 eggs
    1 tsp vanilla
    1/4 tsp salt
    1/4 tsp nutmeg
    2 tbsp butter

With mixer, beat flour milk eggs vanilla salt and nutmeg until smooth. Heat oven to 475 degrees. In cast iron skillet, melt butter. Add sliced apples and fry for 2 to 3 minutes. Pour batter mixture over the fried apples. Bake in the hot oven for 15 mins, then reduce oven heat to 425 and continue baking for 8to 10 minutes. Remove from oven, sprinkle with sugar and cut into wedges. Serve with syrup, jam, whipped cream, and of course, bacon.

SHOOFLY PIE

One can't think about Amish cooking or baking without imaging the sticky, gooey confection known as "shoofly pie." The stories as to how this pie came by its unusual name are as varied as the recipes for the pie. Food historian Don Yoder says, "The key ingredient in this pie is molasses, and prior to refrigeration, it was never available during hot weather due to its perishability. Shoo-fly pie was invented for the U.S. Centennial in 1876, and Pennsylvania Dutch cookbooks from the 1870s and 1880s call it Centennial Cake." Yoder credit's the later incarnation of the name to the Shoofly Molasses Company, but records that such a company ever existed are hard to come by. Another theory that some have floated that has some plausibility is that the "Shoofly" is a variation of an unknown old Pennsylvania German word that was just mangled in translation. And, of course, there's the fun - but improbably - explanation that the pie gets its name from cooks having to shoo the flies away from the pools of molasses that would form on the pie. No matter the pie's origin, it is delicious and it was adopted by Amish cooks because the ingredients were a perfect match for their simple style.

Preheat oven to 400. Prepare 2 empty, unbaked pie crusts.

Crumb Mixture:

    2 c flour
    3/4 c brown sugar
    1/3 c butter
    1/2 tsp nutmeg
    1 tsp cinnamon

Syrup Mixture:

    1 c molasses
    1/2 c brown sugar
    2 eggs
    1 c hot water
    1 tsp baking soda, dissolved in the hot water

Mix crumb ingredients together until crumbs are well formed. In separate bowl, mix syrup ingredients together.

In each empty pie crust, pour 1/2 the syrup mixture. Top with 1/2 crumb mixture, spread evenly. Bake at 400 for 10 mins, then reduce heat to 350 and bake 50 minutes longer. Cool completely before cutting. Serve with whipped cream or ice cream, if you like.

AMISH BEEF STEW

2-3 lbs boneless beef cubes (calculated for 2 lbs.)
2 tablespoons shortening
1 large onion, sliced
4 cups boiling water
1 tablespoon salt
1 tablespoon lemon juice
1 tablespoon sugar
1 tablespoon Worcestershire sauce
1/2 teaspoon pepper
1 1/2 teaspoons paprika
1 dash allspice
1 dash clove
6 carrots, peeled and cut into chunks or 1 lb peeled baby carrot
6 potatoes, peeled and cut into chunks
1/2 cup cold water
1/4 cup flour

Directions

Melt shortening over high heat in a large pot or dutch oven. Add beef cubes and brown over medium heat, stirring occasionally, about 15-20 minutes. Add onions, boiling water, salt, lemon juice, sugar, worcestershire sauce, pepper, paprika, allspice and cloves. Simmer, tightly covered, for about 2 hours, stirring occasionally. Add vegetables and simmer another 30 minutes (covered), or until tender. 6

Note: if your lid is not tight on the pot, you may not have enough liquid left to just about cover everything after you add the vegetables. If this is the case, add more water to barely cover ingredients. Mix cold water and flour together and blend until smooth. Push meat and vegetables to the side of the pot and add flour mixture slowly, incorporating into liquid.

When gravy thickens, stir all ingredients gently to distribute gravy evenly. Simmer another 5 or 10 minutes and enjoy!

WHAT IS CLEAR JEL?

Many of the Amish Cook's pie recipes call for Clear Jel, a product that has caused much confused and conversation with the column community over the years. Here's a primer as to what this thickener is and isn't.

Clear Jel®, a corn starch derivative, is a commercial thickening product used by bakeries and for frozen food. This product is used the same as flour or corn starch. There are two types of Clear Jel® available, "instant" and "regular." "Instant" does not require heat to thicken. The product will thicken once the liquid is added. "Regular," on the other hand, must be heated. This is generally the preferred type to use in products to be canned.

To use Clear Jel® in a hot dish such as gravy, first mix a small amount in cold water, then add gradually to the hot liquid, mixing constantly. Or, mix everything together while cold, and then heat and stir to thicken.

Pies and fillings which have been prepared with Clear Jel® and frozen need to be cooked or baked before serving. If the fillings become "thin" during baking, increase the oven temperature, and shorten the baking time to prevent what is called "oven boil out." This usually is caused by excessive baking at a temperature too low.

Advantages:

- It is clear in color when cooked.
- It has excellent stability.
- It remains smooth.
- It prevents liquid separation and curdling after foods have been frozen.
- Cream sauces, custard, and puddings may be frozen with excellent results.
- It is less expensive than pectin.

- The amount of sugar may be adjusted without losing the jelling capacity.
- Recipes may be doubled, tripled or halved.
- The jam may be frozen or processed in a boiling water bath for 10 minutes.

Hints:

- Using Clear Jel® in making jams and jellies is not an exact science. Many factors influence the quality of the product. It is best to try a small batch and make adjustments before making larger batches.
- Use pint or 1/2 pint jars.
- Any fruit jam or jelly recipe may be used as long as the product is processed for 10 minutes or frozen. Substitute 7 tbsp of Clear Jel® for the pectin in cooked jams and jellies and 3-4 tbsp of Clear Jel® for the pectin in freezer jam recipes.
- For freezer jam follow the jam recipes on this sheet.
- Clear Jel® does not dissolve easily in liquid. To help dissolve the product mix the Clear Jel® with a little sugar before adding to the fruit or juice.

Problem solving:

- Jam is too stiff: To make softer, heat the product and add a little more juice or water, then reprocess.
- Jam is too thin: To make stiffer, heat the product and add more Clear Jel® mixed with a few tbsp of sugar and dissolved in 1/2 cup of the product.

Here are some of the Amish Cook's favorite recipes calling for Clear-Jel:

HOMEMADE BLUEBERRY PIE FILLING

6 quarts of fresh blueberries
6 cups sugar
2 1/4 cup clear gel
7 cups cold water
1 /2 cup lemon juice

Use fresh, ripe blueberries or unsweetened frozen blueberries. Wash and drain if using fresh blueberries. Combine sugar and clear-gel in a large kettle over medium high heat. Add water (blue food coloring can be added here to give the filling even more of a "blue hue." Cook on medium high until mixture thickens and begins to bubble. Add lemon juice and boil one minute, stirring constantly. Fold in berries and then fill sterilized jars up to 1 /2 inch from the top. Adjust lids and process immediately in boiling water for 30 minutes. Store in cool place. Using filling for pies.

HOMEMADE PANCAKE SYRUP

1/4 cup margarine
3 cups brown sugar
3 cups boiling water
1/8 teaspoon salt
1 tablespoon vanilla
1/2 cup clear gel

Melt butter but do not brown. Add sugar, salt, and vanilla. Stir in boiling water. Bring to a good boil. In a separate bowl, mix clear gel with enough water to stir and add slowly to boiling mixture. Boil on low heat for about 20 minutes. Add more thickening if desired before finished boiling.

WHAT IS MILNOT?

When I was sorting through some old recipes of the late Elizabeth Coblentz this morning I stumbled upon one that called for a can of Milnot. I usually try to steer clear of mentioning brand names in the column but I think years ago when I first stumbled on Milnot, I didn't realize it was a brand-name. I just thought it was some ingredient or spice that others maybe had heard of but I hadn't. Ah, what fond memories THAT conjured up. I remember the first time Elizabeth listed that ingredient in her column. I received calls from several grocers asking me what Milnot was? They said some of their customers had been asking for it. I think the column - and newspapers in general - had more influence back then. Today if someone didn't know what Milnot was they'd just Google it. Anyway, for the uninitiated, Milnot is simply a brand name for a particular line of evaporated milk. Elizabeth liked used it in cheesecakes. Milnot shouldn't be confused with sweetened condensed milk, because that is different.

Milnot is sometimes referred to as "filled milk" a skim milk that has been reconstituted with fats, usually vegetable oils from sources other than dairy cows and only exists as evaporated milk. Like pure evaporated milk, filled milk is generally considered unsuitable for drinking because of its particular flavor, but is equivalent to evaporated milk for baking and cooking purposes. Other filled milk products with substituted fat are used to make ice cream, sour cream, and whipping cream, and half and half substitutes among other dairy products. Coconut oil filled milk became a popular cost-saving product sold throughout the United States in the early 20th century. Coconut oil could be cheaply imported, primarily from Far East and this product was able to undercut the market for evaporated and condensed milk. At the time, liquid milk was not widely available or very popular because of the rarity of refrigeration and the problems of transportation and storage.

In 1923, the Congress banned the interstate sale of filled milk "in imitation or semblance of milk, cream, or skimmed milk" via the "Filled Milk Act" of March 4, 1923 in response to intense lobbying by the dairy industry, attempting to protect its market against competition by cheaper foreign fat. Many states also passed bans or restrictions on the sale and production of filled milk products. The issue of filled milk came to the forefront in several notable court cases for violation of the Act by the shipment in interstate commerce of certain packages of "Milnut," a compound of condensed skimmed milk and coconut oil made in imitation or semblance of condensed milk or cream. The indictment stated, in the words of the statute, that Milnut "is an adulterated article of food, injurious to the public health," and that it is not a prepared food product of the type excepted from the prohibition of the Act.

Subsequently, most states have eliminated restrictions on filled milk and several states have gone against the Supreme Court and struck down restrictions on filled milk. Contrary to the declarations of the legislature in reference to the Filled Milk Act, there is no evidence that filled milk, especially as supplemented by Vitamins A and D, as it usually is, is less healthy than normal evaporated milk and there is in fact evidence that the non-saturated fats in the vegetable oils may be more healthy than the milk fat in normal milk products. Currently, filled milk continues to be widely available in supermarkets in the United States as "Milnot," a brand now owned by Smucker's.

AMISH COOK CLASSIC: CHICKEN CORN SOUP

No one seems to know how "Chicken Corn Soup" became such a classic among the Amish, but it has. It's probably just the fact that the ingredients are simple, seasonal staples that most Amish homemakers have on hand. Most Amish women have their own version of chicken corn soup that they make. This is Lovina's recipe

> 2 lbs. cut up chicken
> 5 cups water
> 1 med. onion, chopped
> 2 tbsp. chopped parsley
> 1/2 cup chopped celery
> 2 ccuo corn
> Salt and pepper
> 1 cup flour
> 1 egg, beaten
> 1/4 cup milk

Simmer chicken in boiling water, remove bones and skin. Strain the stock. Return to pot, add onions, celery and corn. Simmer till vegetables are tender. Mix flour with egg and milk. Rub mixture with fork till it crumbles. Drop crumbs in soup. Cook 10 more minutes covered. Serves 3 to 4.

AMISH COOK CLASSIC: HOMEMADE HOT PEPPER BUTTER

This is not a recipe one just breezes through. This is for the die-hard do-it—yourself-er in the kitchen. The recipe isn't terribly complicated, it's just a lot of work, a lot of stinging skin (and eyes if you aren't careful), but the reward is worth the work. This recipe is a classic example of how the Amish have adapted and embraced "new" foods. Hot peppers have gradually found their way into many Amish gardens and this delicious spread is the end result. The sugar "tames" the fiery peppers and you end up with a sweet/hot balanced spread that is delicious on a sandwich or just spread on bread.

42 hot peppers
1 pint of yellow mustard
1 quart of vinegar
6 cups of sugar
1 tablespoon of salt
1 cup flour
1 1/2 cups water

Grind hot peppers, add mustard, vinegar, sugar, and salt and bring to a boil. Make a paste with flour and water and add to boiling mixture and cook five minutes. Pour into pint jars and seal. Makes 7 pints.

AMISH COOK CLASSIC: HOMEMADE RAISIN BREAD

This recipe comes from the archives of The Amish Cook, first featured in the newspaper column back in 1999. Homemade loaves of bread - white, wheat, raisin, sourdough and numerous others - are staples of Amish diets. Try slicing this raisin bread and then coating it with a generous slather of butter while the bread is still hot, you won't be disappointed!

1 1/2 cups milk
1/4 cup sugar
2 teaspoons salt
1/2 cup butter
1 cup unseasoned mashed potatoes
1/2 cup warm water
2 packages yeast
7 1/2 cups flour
1 1/2 cups raisins

Scald milk, remove from heat, and add sugar, salt, butter and mashed potatoes. Let cool. Dissolve yeast in water, then mix with milk. Add raisins and flour. Stir. Let rise in warm place 1 1/2 hours. Divide dough into 2 loaves. Then mix the following separately: 1/2 cup sugar2 teaspoons cinnamon1/2 cup butter or margarine (melted) Then roll the set aside loaves out on a board and put half of butter, sugar and cinnamon mixture on each roll. Roll up as for a jelly roll and pinch edges together. Bake in loaf pans at 350 degrees to 375 degrees for 45 minutes.

RANDOM FAVORITES

TOMATO CUSTARD

I'm not quite sure what to make of this recipe found in the old archives of Elizabeth Coblentz's. There's no explanation as to whether this is a "dessert," an appetizer, or a main dish. When I hear "custard", I immediately think "dessert", but "tomato" doesn't conjure up such images. No explanation whether to chill or to serve warm. And I'm not even sure what a "custard cup" is. This sounds like it must be a very old recipe. But, I'll share her recipe here and you all can try to make sense of it:

    4 pounds ripe tomatoes
    4 eggs, beaten
    1 cup milk
    1 /2 cup sugar
    1 /2 teaspoon salt
    1/ 8 teaspoon nutmeg

Stew tomatoes in own juice (do not add water) and pass through sieve. Cool and add to beaten eggs, milk, and seasoning. Bake in buttered custard cups. Serves 6

HOMEMADE RHUBARB BAKE

This is an interesting recipe I found in my Amish Cook archives from about 5 years ago. Rhubarb is still in season in many locales, so this is one you might want to try.

    Fresh-cut finely chopped rhubarb (as much as you like)
    1/2 cup brown sugar
    2 cups flour
    1 1/2 teaspoon baking powder
    1/2 cup butter or margarine
    2 eggs
    2 3-ounce packages of Jell-O (any flavor you prefer)
    Topping: 1/2 cup butter, 1 cup flour and 1/2 cups sugar

Mix everything except rhubarb and Jell-O together and press into the bottom of a greased 9x13 pan. Cover completely with finely chopped fresh rhubarb. Sprinkle Jell-O powder over rhubarb. Crumb together butter, flour and sugar. Sprinkle on top and bake at 350 until golden and bubbl

BLUEBERRY CAKE

3/4 c. sugar
1/4 c. vegetable oil
1 egg
1/2 c. milk
2 c. flour
2 tsp. baking powder
1/2 tsp. salt
2 c. blueberries, well drained
TOPPING: 1/4 c. butter
1/2 c. sugar
1/3 c. flour
1/2 tsp. Cinnamon

Combine with fork or pastry cutter. Crumble over cake batter. Cream together sugar, oil and egg until lemon colored. Stir in milk. Sift together flour, baking powder and salt and stir into creamed mixture. Gently fold in blueberries. Spread batter into greased and floured 9x9 square pan. Sprinkle with topping. Bake for 45-50 minutes at 375 degrees

AMISH OATMEAL CAKE

1 1/2 cups milk
3 tablespoons melted margarine
1 1/3 cups dark brown sugar
3 eggs, lightly beaten
2/3 cup rolled oats
2/3 cup coconut
1 (9 or 10-inch) unbaked pie shell

Preheat oven to 425 degrees F. Combine all ingredients. Mix thoroughly. Pour in shell. Sprinkle with additional coconut. Bake 10 minutes. Reduce heat to 350 degrees F and bake for 30 minutes or until knife inserted in middle comes out clean.

CLASSIC CUSTARD PIE

1/3 C Sugar
2 Ts Flour
1/2 Ts Salt
3 Eggs
3 C Milk
1/4 Ts Nutmeg
1 9" unbaked pie shell

Combine sugar, flour, salt and eggs and mix until smooth. Heat milk to boiling point. Add 1 cup hot milk to egg mixture. Pour that into the remaining hot milk. Pour into unbaked pie shell. Sprinkle nutmeg over top. Bake at 350 degrees F. for 45-60 minutes.

MAPLE MENNONITE WALNUT CAKE

1/3 cup soft butter or regular margarine
2 eggs
1 cup maple syrup
1 1/4 cups all-purpose white flour
2 teaspoons baking powder
Pinch salt
1 cup walnuts, chopped not too fine

Beat together butter, eggs, and syrup. This will look curdled don't worry. Sift together flour, baking powder, and salt, and stir in gradually. Beat with whisk until smooth fold in walnuts.

Pour into a greased square pan and bake at 350 degrees F for about 25 to 30 minutes or until done. Let cool before icing with a maple butter icing.

SUMMER SALAD

2 cups raw spinach, finely chopped
1 thinly sliced peeled cucumber
4 green onions, chopped
1/2 cup sliced radishes
2 cups cottage cheese
1 cup sour cream
2 teaspoons fresh or bottled lemon juice
1/2 teaspoon salt
1/4 teaspoon freshly ground pepper
Paprika, to taste
1/2 cup minced fresh parsley

Wash the spinach the day before, then wrap it in a cloth and refrigerate it overnight.

Chop the spinach, add the cucumber, onions and radishes, then toss lightly. Arrange in a wooden salad bowl and place a mound of cottage cheese in the middle.

Blend the sour cream with the lemon juice, salt and pepper and pour over the salad. Sprinkle the paprika in the middle and the parsley all around. Toss when ready to serve.

This is a very good meal in itself, but it's even better when served with thin slices of lightly buttered black bread.

HOME & HEALTH

For a sore throat...
Stick your tongue out as far as possible and count to 30. Your throat will feel better.

To soothe burns...
Rub prepared yellow mustard on your burns, this will give relief.

To rid your home of ants...

This is a safe solution to get rid of ants if you have small children in the house. Sprinkle problem area with cinnamon or cayenne pepper. The ants will never come back.

To wash windows...

Get one pint of water and add one tablespoon of ammonia to it. Many use this to wash their windows.

FLOOR FINISH

If you want your floor stained, do that first. Once the stain is completely dry, mix

> 1 part raw linseed oil
> 1 part white vinegar
> 1 part turpentine.

Apply to floor. This finish lasts years and can be freshened by using more of the same mixture

HOMEMADE FURNITURE POLISH

Use 1 part white vinegar to 3 parts virgin olive oil. Mix well. Apply with a soft, clean cloth

Chapter 7

AMISH THE AMISH COOK

ASK THE AMISH COOK

GARDENING

In one of her columns, Elizabeth mentions "winter onions." When do you pull winter onions? Do you pull the large onions or the small ones? Do I only do this in the spring?

NEED ANSWER TO ABOVE QUESTION HERE

What is the proper way to freeze garden-grown vegetables?

We only freeze certain items, others just don't freeze well. Strawberries, raspberries and cherries freeze well. We roll them in sugar and seal them in empty 2 to 3 quart plastic ice cream containers. These seal well. Other fruits, like peaches and apples, don't freeze so well, so we just can those or eat them fresh.

Vegetables such as radishes and hot peppers just don't seem to freeze well, but green beans and corn keep nicely in the ice-box. We steam green beans and corn first in a kettle, let it cool, and then seal and freeze it. These are good ways to keep certain fruits and vegetables, but for most of our produce we home-can it. It keeps this way much longer, and fresher.

Did Lovina plant any wax (yellow) beans this year and if so how are they doing in this weather? Mine are ready to can but not the yellow color they are supposed to be. (they are mostly yellow with a hint of green). Cat - Bellefontaine, Ohio

Lovina: I plant some each year, they can well and the family seems to enjoy them!

I would like to know about which canning methods that Lovina uses. I haven't seen mention of a pressure canner, so am thinking that she uses water bath method for everything. Any information appreciated. Caryl - Madison, Wisconsin

Lovina: I use water bath for fruits and vegetables, pressure canner for meats.

Does Lovina keep records of how much she harvests from her gardens or how much she cans? If so, that would be interesting to know. Chuck - Alexandria, Louisiana

Lovina: I don't keep records, but each spring I'll go down to the cellar and count how many cans of each item I have left, that way I know which items we are eating the most of so I can adjust my spring planting accordingly.

Please ask Lovina if there are any heirloom varieties of veggies she's interested in trying, or maybe some her mom planted that she hasn't been able to find. I am a member of Seedsavers Exchange, and I would be delighted to help her out if you can get me the name of the veggie or fruit. Meg - Florida

Lovina: Thank you for the generous offer! But I usually can find what I need to plant each year.

I have a question for Lovina. In the last weekly column, she said she was going to pull or harvest her winter onions. Find out when she will plant them again, and when she harvests them what she does to the little onions on the tops. I have never raised them before, and have about 30 set. I have just let them "go" in the garden and don't want to lose them.

Lovina: I have never let them go. I always pull them in late July. Mom always said to not let the August sun hit the onions, so I pull them.

Do you have any suggestions for keeping deer from eating all my flowers and bushes in my back yard? I have a 4' fence between the woods behind my property and my backyard, but they must jump it as I see hoof prints and my flowers are chewed to a stubble. Please help if you can. Thanks so much. - Sue in Cincinnati

We rid our garden of deer - which are plentiful in this area - by sprinkling mothballs generously throughout the area we wish to protect. The deer don't like mothballs so it keeps them away!

You once had a "fly catcher" recipe in one of your columns. I know you needed a 2-liter pop bottle, "vinegar, sugar and water, but I forget the amounts. It worked great and I would like to use it again ." Charlene - Harrisonburg, VA

Take a 2-liter pop bottle (we use green like 7-Up or Sprite) and fill with 1 cup sugar, 1 cup vinegar, and banana peelings. Fill up with water 3 /4 full. Hang on the lower branch of a tree. Be patient, because it takes a good week or two for the trap to begin working. But once insects start coming in, they come in bunches. Once they fly into the bottle, they are done for. Works great for ridding your yard of insects.

How deep must rhubarb be planted and what tips can you give me for growing large healthy rhubarb plants. Marsha - Arcola, IL

It depends on how big the plants are. You just need to plant them deep enough so that the roots are covered.

Do you have any suggestions on how to control Mexican bean beetles in the garden? Each year my beans are ravaged by these pests. How about Japanese beetle larvae in the yard, prior to them hatching into beetles? I am considering Milky spore, but I have a large area and I'm concerned about my wife's allergies. Terry - Springfield, Ohio

I always like to grow marigold flowers in my garden. Keeps a lot of stuff out. The insect pests just don't like the marigolds. I put rows through my garden. Other Amish women I know put rows through her garden and then plants them surrounding the outside border of her whole garden. Seems to keep all kinds of pests away. I hope this helps.

COOKING

I know that Lovina is horribly busy, but does she have a hobby that she "indulges" in? And what is her favorite recipe or favorite thing to eat? - Suzanne - Kalamazoo, Michigan

Lovina: "Love to quilt and read in my spare time, which I hardly ever have. Ha! And I'll eat anything from the garden, but homemade cinnamon rolls are probably my favorite food to make myself."

Hello! Could you please send a recipe for your fried green tomatoes? I read about it in the paper and lost the article -Dee - South Bend, Indiana

Fried Green Tomatoes is another spring favorite in this household. My mother used to make it almost every day during the summer months, and it's something that I fix a lot too in my household. My husband Ben was especially fond of them. All you do is slice them, about 1/2 inch thick slices, and roll them in flour so they are coated. Season with salt and pepper and fry in a greased skillet on medium high until golden brown on each side. Enjoy!

Do you have a recipe for potato puffs and barbecue chicken. We visited a restaurant and they had both items and were very good. We enjoy reading your recipes every week ... also a woman wrote in asking about the noodle factory ... it was shown on the food network and is located in Topeka, Indiana

Do you mean like fried potato patties? We take leftover mashed potatoes and shape into patties and then fry them in a greased skillet until golden brown on each side. Makes for a good meal. As far as barbecuing chicken, that is a summer favorite here. My son-in-law, Joe, often does the barbecuing. We make a barbecue sauce by getting a quart pan and filling it 3 /4 of the way with apple cider vinegar and then add 1/4 pound of oleo. Season with salt and pepper and heat until steaming warm. Then baste chicken with it and barbecue. Has a good taste.

There was once a recipe in The Amish Cook column for one-hour yeast rolls. I have lost the recipe, do you have it. Mary - Lancaster, Kentucky

Amish Cook's Editor's Answer: Mary, you weren't alone. Several people misplaced this quick, tasty roll recipe that appeared in a past column. I am including it below

ONE HOUR ROLLS

2 cakes of yeast (or 2 packages of dry yeast)
1/4 cup of lukewarm water
1 1/4 cup of milk
3 tablespoons of sugar
1/2 teaspoon of salt
4 tablespoons of butter
3 cups of flour

Dissolve yeast in water. Milk, sugar, salt, and butter should be put into a pan over the oven and heated to lukewarm. Add yeast and flour and stir until blended. Put in a warm place for 15 minutes. Turn out on a floured board and press to 1 inch thickness. Cut out circles. Fold dough over bits of butter. Place on greased cookie sheet. Let rise 15 minutes and bake 10 minutes at a 350 degree oven.

I've tried and tried to make potato pancakes like my mother used to make without a recipe, but I just can't get them to taste or the texture the same. Perhaps it's just my childhood memory gone awry, but all of the recipes I look up and try out taste too much like hashbrowns. Hers had a heavy hotcake texture, using grated raw potatoes, flour and egg, but I can't get it right. We enjoyed these on cold rainy nights with butter and maple syrup. Can you help me? Sharon - DuPont, Washington

I am not sure if her answer is what you were seeking, but we used to make pancake patties out of mashed potatoes. Mother would make them frequently. We would take mashed potatoes - say you had 1 quart of leftover mashed potatoes - and add 3 eggs to them and stir well, very well. Then we would shape them into patties and fry in a skillet of hot grease until golden brown on both sides. The more eggs you add the thicker they will be. Some people also add 1 tablespoon of flour, but I never do, the eggs hold them together. Delicious!

I have a question is oleo considered margarine or butter? I am making Toffee. Thank you!! Linda, Shawnee, Kansas

It's margarine.

My great grandmother was Dunkard in Lancaster County Pennsylvania. Is this a form of Amish? She made a recipe of Schnitz and Knepf? Do you know what this is? Bonnie - Danville, Illinois

Editor's Answer: Dunkers (sometimes called Dunkards or German Baptists) obtain the name of their faith from their practice of full-body immersion in water when baptized. The Dunkers are often confused with the Amish because their dress is similar. Men wear long beards and simple clothing, while women wear bonnets and hand-sewn dresses. Dunkers do embrace more modern technology, though, than the Amish. Dunkers will drive cars and own radios, for instance. They still resist some modern conveniences like television and computers in an effort to maintain a simpler lifestyle.

The Amish Cook is quite familiar with the food dish you mentioned. Some Amish used to have a "drying house" outside where they would dry apples for schnitz apples. Hope this recipe is what you were looking for:

SCHNITZ AND KNEPF

1 quart dried apples
2 tablespoons brown sugar
1 teaspoon salt
1 egg (beaten)
1 /2 cup milk

3 lbs end of smoked ham
2 cups flour
4 teaspoons baking powder
3 tablespoons melted butter

In a big pot, cover apples and ham with water and simmer over a low heat for 2 hours. Add brown sugar and simmer 1 hour longer. Prepare dumplings: Mix flour, baking powder and salt. Then in a separate bowl, stir egg, butter and milk. Add to flour mixture. Drop by tablespoon into simmering ham and apples. Cover tightly and cook 15 minutes without lifting lid. Serves 8 to 10

I have been working with my grandmother's noodle recipe for some time. I use her proportions (3 eggs, 2 c. flour, 1/2 t. salt). Mixing and rolling are not a problem; the result is. I am successful only part of the time. Sometimes they are dry and sometimes I can't get them to dry. Before she passed, my grandmother talked about doing noodles at the "right time." My mother said that she wasn't sure, but she thought it had to do with humidity and time of year. Is this true? Thank you so much. Cheryl, Columbus, Oh

I usually like to make my noodles in the spring and fall. The flies aren't so thick then and the temperature and humidity are usually perfect. I usually make my noodles in late April or early May or in October. When you are done, lay them out on a table to dry. Make sure they aren't too crowded, that they have room to dry. [Editor's note: The Amish Cook also said if your dough is too wet, add a bit more flour, if it is too dry, add a bit more water.

My grandmother's maiden name was Metzger and her father was an Elder in the Old Order Dunkard (German Baptist) church near North Manchester, IN where I grew up. She used to make a soup called rivels soup and I've been looking for a recipe for it. Do you have one? Larry, Costa Mesa, CA

When times were especially tough, Mom would make rivvels. Rivvels are little rice-sized pieces of dough, served in soup. The soup sort of resembles a gravy. Mother would take dough and rub it through her hands and drop it into a boiling broth. Instead of having noodles, she would fix a broth soup, like rivvel soup. The rivvel soup tastes like a gravy. Mom would fix this a lot on Saturday, which would be a good inexpensive meal before a larger, better meal on Sunday. Here is the recipe. I hope this helps!

RIVVELS

1 quart beef broth
1 egg, well-beaten
1 cup flour
1/2 teaspoon salt

Heat the broth in a medium-sized pot until boiling. Combine flour, salt and egg in a bowl until mixture is crumbly. Rub the dough through your hands into the boiling broth. Cook about 10 minutes on medium heat. Rivvels will look like boiled rice when cooked. You may also use milk instead of broth if you wish.

When you find blood in your raw eggs what does that mean and should you use it in cooking? Jennifer - Big Rapids, Michigan

I never use the eggs if they have blood in them.

Some of the Amish Cook's recipes, like one for banana bread, call for sour milk. What do you mean by that? Please explain. Thank you! Linda - Newton, New Jersey

Let milk sour and if not on hand you can add a small amount (tablespoon per cup) of vinegar to the milk to get the same taste. Adding vinegar will sour the milk. Sour milk makes a good taste in some breads, it gets thick and makes them moist. At home, mother would let the milk sour and skim the cream off the top for a homemade sour cream. Never drink sour milk, but good for baking.

I have seen Clear-Jel mentioned in several Amish Cook recipes. What is this?

Editor's Answer: This is a thickening used in pie fillings. Many Amish women order Clear-Jel from catalogues or buy it from small country stores. Clear-Jel can also be used in jams, preserves, etc.

Following is some information from: Reynolds, Susan and Paulette Williams. So Easy to Preserve. Bulletin 989. Cooperative Extension Service, the University of Georgia. Revised by Elizabeth Andress and Judy Harrison (1999.

Obtain your Clear Jel before assembling the fruit and other ingredients to make these pie fillings. In most areas, mail order is the only source. Clear Jel may be mail ordered from either Home Canning Essentials (Alltrista), 1-800-392-2575 or Sweet Celebrations, 1-800-328-6722. Call for prices and shipping and handling costs. There are about 3 cups in 1 pound of Clear Jel. The fruit pie filling recipes take about 1 to 2^1 cups Clear Jel per 6 to 7 quarts of pie filling. For more information on home canning, contact your local Extension agent.

I have been looking for a recipe for tomato gravy which my mother made with squirrel and rabbit. Would you have such a recipe? I really enjoy your column in the Monday editions of The South Bend Tribune. Fred - Buchanan, Michigan

That is a family favorite. When the children we small, we served this all the time. Place 1 quart of tomato juice in a kettle and bring to a boil. Then add a thickening of 2 tablespoons flour mixed with milk and add to the boiling water, stirring constantly until it boils and is thickened. It may be served with bread, toast, or crackers. I made this a lot while the children were young for dinner as they liked it very well. Season with salt and pepper to your taste. Some like a little sugar added to it. So do it however you like it.

CULTURAL QUESTIONS

Without phones, faxes, cells, etc. how do the Amish communicate with one another? Sharon - South Bend, Indiana

Sharon, you ask a good question. The Amish don't have the luxuries that you and I have to communicate. Briefly, The Amish rely on the old-fashioned word-of-mouth driven grapevine to community. Word of a death, for instance, can spread like wildfire as gossip is traded after church and everyone scatters in different directions. One of the more reliable methods of communicating is through "The Budget" this is an Amish newspaper published in Sugarcreek, Ohio and mailed to most Amish families through the USA. There are "scribes" stationed in almost every community. They'll write in the latest news in their community (births, weddings, funny stories) and then they'll be published in "The Budget." This way an Amish person in Yoder, Kansas can find out what is going on in a faraway Amish community like Lancaster, Pennsylvania. The Amish also rely heavily on the dying art of old-fashioned letter writing and a U.S. postage stamp.

I was wondering if it is possible for non amish to be pen pals with someone amish?? Lynda, Cartersville, Georgia

Editor's Answer: As you can imagine, many people write to The Amish Cook wanting her to be pen pals with them. She just gets too much mail to try to do that. Sometimes an Amish person will correspond with a non-Amish one, although pen pals between Amish people are far more common. This is a tough one because the fact is, non-Amish people find the Amish a lot more fascinating than they find us. So the interest level often just is not there. Throw in the fact that the Amish lifestyle, by its very nature, stresses as little contact with the outside world as possible, and finding an Amish is even tougher.

An Amish newspaper called Die Botschaft (in German, this means "The News") sometimes has classified ads from Amish people seeking pen pals. That's the best place to connect. For a copy, mail ($5 should be enough to get a copy) to: Die Botschaft, 200 Hazel St, Lancaster, PA 17608 or call them at 717-392-1321 for an exact price for one copy.

Another source would be The Budget, the unofficial newspaper of the Amish-Mennonite community. You can put a classified ad in there seeking a pen-pal, or sometimes there are even Amish who will have ads of their own in there seeking a pen-pal simply as a means of cultural exchange. The address and phone number of the Budget is:

Budget Publishing
134 Factory St NE
Sugarcreek, OH 44681-9301
Phone: (330)852-4634

I read your column in the South Bend Tribune every week and I enjoy it so much. I have a question: My husband and I have noticed when we travel that the lamps that the Amish use are so much brighter than the ones we buy in the store. Since our electric fails quite often I would like to know if they are a lot different and if so where in Indiana can we purchase them? I'd sure appreciate it if you can help me...Thank you so much! Lorainne - South Bend, Indiana

Editor's answer: I have seen two main types of lighting in Amish homes at night. Believe it or not, the lanterns many Old Order Amish use are nothing more than Coleman kerosene lamps that you can purchase at almost any outdoors store. They do use more decorative kerosene lamps with glass globes for light lighting, say on an end table. But for the really bright lights that you see while driving by an Amish house at night, those are just Coleman kerosene lamps. And you are right, they are also bright. The light in an Amish house at night, if it has a Coleman kerosene lamp, is brighter than our electric lamps by far.

You might also be seeing gas lamps, but you really can't buy these. Some Amish homes, especially in your area, light their homes using gas ceiling lamps that are connected to a piped in source. These, too, are very bright!

We ate at the Der Dutchman Restaurant in Sarasota, FL last evening and were wondering how the Amish can operate all their restaurants if they do not use electricity?   Barbara - Inverness, Florida

Editor's Answer: Der Dutchman is a chain of "Amish style" restaurants. I believe there are 3 locations, one in Mansfield, Ohio; one in Waynesville, Ohio, and one in Sarasota, Florida. All restaurants are sprawling restaurant/conference centers will huge bakeries and gift shops. While the owners of these restaurants are of Amish background, they are not Old Order Amish. You are correct, an Old Order Amish person would unlikely be able to operate such an establishment without violating their faith. I have had the occasion to dine at Der Dutchman. The restaurants serve good, hearty Amish-style food, but they fall short of being authentic.

This question has two related parts: First, I have noticed in the book "The Best of the Amish Cook, Volume I" that Elizabeth wrote often early in the book about quilting that she and her girls had been doing. In later columns, there has been little, if any, mention about quilting. Is this because the girls all have their requisite number of quilts for their hope chests? Or is it just not mentioned anymore?

Second, again about sewing: Elizabeth and her girls often cut out and sew clothes for the family. I am wondering what they use for patterns. Is there such a thing as patterns for "Amish clothes" or do they know how to do it without patterns? If so, can you share this method with us?   Carol, Homosassa, FL

Editor's Answer: Some Amish women sew quilts to sell so they are always quilting. Many Amish families, though, have a set number of quilts to make, and then they are done. Elizabeth Coblentz made 16 quilts and 16 knotted quilts, two for each of her children. In addition, she made eight bed comforters. Most of these were sewn in the early 90s. Once completed, she didn't do much quilting unless invited to a quilting bee. Each child treasures the homemade quilts from their mother and will keep them for life.

The pattern question was an interesting one. Most Amish women use patterns for their caps, bonnets, and the top portion of their dresses. Shirts, skirts and sleeves are just made by measuring the fabric. The patterns are very simple cut-outs, usually made from freezer paper and stored in a folder.

There are some online retailers that specialize in Amish clothing. I recommend: http://www.friendspatterns.net/

Is the Amish Cook column carried anywhere near the Quad Cities?

Barbara

Editor's answer: No. The closest newspaper to the Quad Cities to carry the column is Quincy, Illinois. Call the editors at the Quad Cities Times or the Rock Island Argus and ask them to carry the column.

A reader asked about the windmills that often dot the countryside in Amish country. The windmills operate water pumps. The reader wanted to know where she could obtain such a windmill.

Editor's Answer: I asked an Amish woman about her windmill and she said that the windmill at her farm was put up decades ago and the company that put it up - using 8 men to erect the tall structure - is no longer in existence. A good place to find companies that do business among the Amish is The Budget, the newspaper of the Amish community, which features writers and advertisers. To obtain a copy, contact:

Budget Publishing
134 Factory St NE,
Sugarcreek, OH 44681-9301
Phone: (330)852-4634

I work with an agency that produces materials for people who are blind or visually impaired. Over 70 percent of our staff is also blind or visually impaired, and they all use very hi-tech devices to get along in their daily lives. Our office uses such things as talking computers, high magnification devices, and computerized embossers to produce the necessary Braille material. Several of us are ardent fans of The Amish Cook and we have been wondering how people who are Amish and are also in need of such special devices cope with their physical limitations would fare in their culture. Carol

Editor's answer: I took your question to The Amish Cook, because I found it interesting. Elizabeth Coblentz commented that there are Amish people that she knows who are blind. They read with standard Braille texts. Elizabeth also told me: "A first cousin of mine was blinded at age 12. He makes wastebaskets to sell. Even though he has no sight, his surroundings are so familiar to him that he is able to walk out to the barn and do the milking without help."

Elizabeth says that, like any Amish person who is afflicted with a physical limitation, the people usually finds themselves surrounded by a web of support, both family and community. I am always awed by this sense of community that leaves no one out

10 NEVER-PUBLISHED CLASSICS FROM THE ARCHIVES

At the time of Elizabeth Coblentz's passing (she was the original Amish Cook columnist) we were working on a new cookbook. We didn't get very far, but she had provided me with many recipes to begin to get the new book into shape. It was going to spotlight very traditional Amish cooking. Here are 10 recipes from that effort, that have not been published online or in any of our books - until now. Enjoy!

Amish Cinnamon Bread Recipe

    2 T. yeast
    3/4 c. sugar
    4 T. cinnamon
    1/2 c. raisins (optional)
    3/4 c. warm water

Let stand 5 to 10 minutes.

Mix in:

    1/2 c. sugar
    2 T. salt
    1/2 c. vegetable oil
    4 c. warm water
    3 c. flour

Stir until smooth, then knead in approximately 9 cups flour, or until smooth and elastic. Let rise trice, keeping covered at all times. Divide into loaves;

let rise. Bake at 400° for 20 minutes. When done, make a glaze of a small amount of water and powdered sugar and drizzle on top of loaves.

HAMBURGER CORN NOODLE CASSEROLE

11/2 lb. ground beef
1 medium onion
11/2 teaspoons salt
1/4 teaspoon pepper
11/2 cups corn
1 can cream of mushroom soup
1 can cream of chicken soup
1 cup sour cream
2 cups dry noodles

Mix all ingredients and put in casserole. Bake at 350° F until noodles are done. Very tasty!
Serves 8

SOUR CREAM PANCAKES

2 c. flour
4 t. baking powder
2 eggs
1 c. (8 oz.) sour cream
1/4 c. sugar
1/2 t. salt
1 1/2 c. milk
1/3 c. butter, melted

Combine dry ingredients in a bowl. In another bowl, beat the eggs. Add milk, sour cream and butter; mix well. Stir into dry ingredients just until moistened. Pour batter on hot griddle or skillet and cook.

FLUFFY DOUGHNUTS

3 eggs, beaten
2 c. warm water
4 T. dry yeast
6 c. flour
1 T. salt
1/2 c. granulated sugar
1/2 c. vegetable oil
1 to 2 tsp. lemon &/or vanilla flavoring (opt.)

Beat eggs in a medium bowl. Dissolve yeast in water; mix with eggs. Add rest of ingredients, mixing well. Put into a covered bowl and let rise until doubled. Roll out on a lightly-floured surface and cut with a donut cutter. Let donuts rise until doubled. Deep-fat-fry at 375°.

Cool, then dip into a glaze made of:

2 c. powdered sugar
1/3 c. milk
1 tsp. vanilla

These stay soft and good for a few days.

Variation: For something different, try dipping donut tops into this chocolate glaze:

4 c. powdered sugar
1/2 c. cocoa
1/4 tsp. salt
1/3 c. hot water
1/3 c. butter or margarine, melted
1 tsp. vanilla flavoring

Grape Salad Recipe

8 oz. cream cheese
1 1/2 c. powdered sugar
1 c. Cool Whip
1 c. sour cream

Mix all together and add as many grapes as you wish.

KANSAS SUGAR COOKIES

1 c. sugar
1 c. powdered sugar
1 c. butter
1 c. oil
2 eggs
1 tsp. almond extract
1 tsp. salt
1 tsp. cream of tartar
1 tsp. baking soda
4 1/2 c. flour
1 T. vanilla

Directions

Creams sugars and butter; beat in eggs and oil. Add the rest of the ingredients. Refrigerate overnight. Form dough into small balls, roll in sugar and place on baking sheet. Flatten balls with a glass dipped in sugar. Bake at 350 degrees for 12 minutes.

RHUBARB DRINK

Ingredients

4 lb. rhubarb
4 qt. water
2 c. sugar
1 c. pineapple juice
1 (6oz) can frozen orange juice

Directions

Boil rhubarb and water until soft.
Drain and add the remaining ingredients in given order.
Put into jars and can.
For a refreshing snack drink, add 7-up

AMISH STUFFED CHICKEN

4 skinless boneless chicken breast halves
2 skinless chicken thighs
1/4 cup pistachio nuts
2 tablespoons whipping cream
1/4 teaspoon salt
1/4 teaspoon pepper salt and pepper
1 tablespoon butter -- melted paprika

Preheat oven to 375 degrees and lightly grease a shallow baking dish. Debone chicken thighs and place meat in a food processor. Process until coarsely ground. Add pistachio nuts, cream and 1/4 teaspoon each of salt and pepper. Process until well combined. Set aside. Place each breast half between two sheets of plastic wrap and flatten to 1/8 inch thick. season with salt and pepper. Place 1/4 of the thigh mixture on each breast and roll up, tucking in the ends. Secure with toothpicks. place rolls in prepared baking dish, brush with melted butter and sprinkle with paprika. Bake until interior temperature is 165 degrees, about 30 - 35 minutes.

Meanwhile prepare the Cider Cream Sauce. In a medium saucepan combine chicken stock, apple juice and vermouth. Bring to a boil, reduce heat slightly and gently boil until reduced to 1/2 cup, about 15 - 20 minutes. Add whipping cream. Return to boiling, reduce heat and gently boil until slightly thickened, about 5 - 7 minutes.

Remove chicken roll from oven and place on serving plates. Spoon Cider Cream Sauce over chicken rolls and serve.

AMISH WACKY CAKE

2 cups sugar
2 teaspoons baking soda
3 cups flour
3/4 cup Crisco oil
6 tablespoons Hershey's Cocoa
2 tablespoons vinegar
2 teaspoons salt
2 cups cold water
1 teaspoons vanilla

Instructions

Heat oven to 350°. Place all ingredients, except 1 cup of the water, into a bowl. Stir until smooth then add the rest of the water. Stir well. Pour batter into a 9"x13" cake pan. Bake 30 to 35 minutes. May be eaten plain or iced with a butter icing.

COUNTRY SAUSAGE

2 lbs sausage
2 lbs tomatoes, skinned & seeded, or 2 large cans tomatoes;
4 medium to large carrots;
2 small to medium turnips;
4 onions chopped
3 stalks celery
4 leeks
1 bay leaf
2 tbsp chopped parsley
salt & pepper to taste
1/2 c stock (beef, vegetable or chicken)

Clean vegetables and cut in 1 inch pieces. In large saucepan, add cut vegetables, stock & herbs. Bring to boil and cook for 5 or 6 minutes. Add sausage, cover and simmer 1 hour.

Serve with homemade bread or rolls.

Easy Cleaning Tips

Fill a small bowel with potted plant charcoal and place it in refrigerator.

An open box of baking soda in the fridge will absorb odors for 6 weeks.

A little vanilla poured on a piece of cotton and placed in fridge will eliminate odors.

To prevent mildew from forming, wipe with vinegar.

Use a glycerine-soaked cloth to wipe sides and shelves. Future spills wipe up easily.

Sinks

For a sparkling white sink, place paper towels across the bottom and saturate with bleach. Let set for 30+ min.

Rub stainless steel sinks with lighter fluid if rust marks appear.

Use a cloth dampened with rubbing alcohol to remove water spots from stainless steel.

Spots on stainless may also be removed with white vinegar.

Club soda will shine up stainless steel in a jiffy.

Remove rust from tin pie pans by dipping a potato in cleaning powder and scouring.

OUT OF THE MOUTHS OF BABES.....

The Amish Cook often receives mail from schoolchildren. This batch of questions came from third-graders at National Trail Middle School in Preble County, Ohio. It's always cute and interesting to look at topics through the eyes of innocence! Some of the questions are just fun to  *read in themselves, some are just statements from the children. We did provide actual answers to a few of the questions! The letters were actually directed towards 12-year-old Verena, so the children were writing to an age-mate.*

I would like to know how you came up with that article. What else do you help your Mom? How can you live without TV and video games?

I love video games and TV. I do karate. It's very fun. My favorite food is ice cream. I can eat it 24/7!

My parents and I like to go motorcyle riding in the summer. It's a lot of fun. You feel the wind blow by your arms - Ashley

I'm wondering if you have lights. Because I have a lot of trouble when the lights go out. And I'm just wondering: does your Mom make cold ice cream like the stores? And does your Mom like ice cream? Does your Mom make your clothes? - Lillie

LOVINA: We gas-powered lights, they really provide a bright light for us to read by! And, yes, homemade ice cream is a favorite among the children in this household!

I have a few questions for you. If this offends you, well, sorry. Do you ever get bored at your house? Do you have electricity? And what do you do when you're not at school. Sorry. I'm not trying to be pushy. Well I hope you get back to me. - Kenzie

LOVINA: Never a boring or dull moment around this house with eight children, two adults, and plenty of livestock!

How have you been doing? My name is Jeremiah. Do you like animals? I have three dogs and one monkey. How is it having no electricity? How is it riding in a buggy? I think riding in a car would be a lot better. They are faster than a horse and buggy. Do you like waffles? Waffles are one of my most favorite foods. - Jeremiah

How was your day? I have to ask you, do you do all the household chores for your mother because you love her or because she tells you to do them? I'm very glad I read your article because I like to see different points of view from children my age. I know you guys don't have TV so what do you do in your spare time? - Taylor

LOVINA: We love to play board games, read, sing, and just spend time together as a family!

I have a couple of questions for you. I was wondering what do you normally eat and do you like living without electricity? Also what do you usually do after you're done with your homework?

Hi. I think your life is interesting. Do you like your name, Verena? I have never heard that name before. I am 11-years-old. I am a third child....Nick

I heard your Mom is a great cook. Is that true? She has to be. I tried one of her cookie recipes and they were good. Does she have another cookie recipe? How is farm life? I bet good... Christina

How do you like riding buggies? I have two horses. They are the type horses that pull wagons, buggies, and things that are made to be pulled by horses. We hook up the horses in the spring, summer, and fall. The winter is too cold. When we hook up the horse I'm so excited. When we get on the wagon and start to go I love the smell of the fresh cut grass. I love fresh cut grass because it smells like watermelon and watermelon is one of my favorite fruit. – Danielle

Made in the USA
Middletown, DE
28 October 2023

41447001R00091